The Complete Corporate Guide:

Incorporate in Any State

By Michael Spadaccini, Esq.

The Oasis Press® / PSI Research
Central Point, Oregon

Published by The Oasis Press®
© 2002 by Michael Spadaccini, Esq.

This publication is designed to provide accurate and authoritative information
in regard to the subject matter covered. It is sold with the understanding that the
publisher is not engaged in rendering legal, accounting, or other professional
service. If legal advice or other expert assistance is required, the services of a
competent professional person should be sought.
> — *from a declaration of principles jointly adopted by a committee of*
> *the American Bar Association and a committee of publishers.*

Book designer: Constance C. Dickinson
Editor: Vickie Reierson
Compositor: Jan Olsson
Book cover: J. C. Young

Please direct any comments, questions, or suggestions regarding this book to
The Oasis Press®/ PSI Research:

> Editorial Department
> P.O. Box 3727
> Central Point, OR 97502
> (541) 245-6502
> FAX (541) 245-6505
> info@psi-research.com *(email)*

The Oasis Press® is a Registered Trademark of Publishing Services, Inc.,
an Oregon corporation doing business as PSI Research.

Library of Congress Cataloging-in-Publication Data

Spadaccini, Michael, 1964–
    The complete corporate guide : incorporate in any state / Michael Spadaccini.
      p. cm.
    Includes index.
    ISBN 1-55571-618-0 (paper)
    1. Incorporation—United States. 2. Incorporation—United States—Forms. 3. Corporation
law—United States—Forms. I. Title.
KF1420.Z9 S66 2001
346.73'06622—dc21   2001034358

Printed in the United States of America
First Edition 10 9 8 7 6 5 4 3 2 1

♻ Printed on recycled paper when available.

Table of Contents

Introduction

This book is intended for anyone interested in incorporating a business in any state, or the District of Columbia. If you're an entrepreneur, businessperson, manager, lawyer, or accountant, this book gives you the tools to plan, organize, form, operate, and maintain a basic for-profit corporation. The book provides a basic understanding of the law surrounding business organizations, such as sole proprietorships, partnerships, limited liability companies, and corporations. Each business form is explained in simple terms and a list of advantages and disadvantages for each help you to determine which is best for your business.

Once you've decided which type of corporation you will form, this book lays out the incorporation process in a clear, step-by-step format. Some of the corporate mysteries you'll learn include:

- How to select a state for incorporation;
- How to select a name;
- How to conduct a search for prior business names and trademarks;
- How to choose and elect directors, a registered agent, and officers; and
- How to file your corporate papers.

This book will then assist you with the ongoing responsibilities of running a corporation, such as organizing annual and special meetings of directors and shareholders; taking corporate actions by written consent; drafting corporate minutes; reporting and paying annual franchise and corporate income taxes; and meeting periodic reporting requirements.

To ensure you get a better understanding and feel for corporate paperwork and documentation, a hefty part of the book features model or sample documents for you to review and modify to suit your needs. More than 20 sample forms and documents are in Appendix A. These model documents also appear at the website, www.learnaboutlaw.com, and are available for download in popular word-processing formats.

Appendix B provides corporate reference information for all 50 states and the District of Columbia. Each reference table includes contact information for the secretary of states' offices (or other appropriate office) for the filing of incorporation papers; the amount of incorporation filing fees; links to model forms; and information on periodic reporting and tax requirements. Appendix C offers a glossary of terms.

Understand, of course, this book cannot possibly serve as a substitute for the legal advice of a qualified attorney or accountant tailored to your specific needs. The information here is not intended as specific legal advice; rather, it is intended as a broad educational overview.

Chapter 1

Choosing the Right Business Organization

The most common forms of business structures in use in the United States are the sole proprietorship, general partnership, limited liability partnership, limited partnership, limited liability company (LLC), and the corporation. Each form has advantages and disadvantages in complexity, ease of set-up, cost, liability protection, periodic reporting requirements, operating complexity, and taxation. Choosing the right business form requires a delicate balancing of competing considerations.

Regardless of which business you choose, you can reasonably expect that your state and local jurisdiction will carry licensing and filing responsibilities for your business. Local licensing rules will vary from jurisdiction to jurisdiction, but expect more stringent requirements in cities. Some requirements to watch for include:

- City and/or county business license;
- City and/or county local taxation;
- City and/or county land use and zoning laws;
- State sales tax registration and filings; and
- Registration for certain industries.

The Sole Proprietorship

The sole proprietorship is the simplest business form under which you can operate a business, but the sole proprietorship is not a legal entity. It simply refers to a natural person who owns the business and is personally responsible for its debts.

The sole proprietorship is a popular business form due to its simplicity, ease of set-up, and nominal cost. If you are a sole proprietor, you need only register your name and secure local licenses, and the sole proprietorship is ready for business. A distinct disadvantage, however, is that as owner of a sole proprietorship, you remain personally liable for all the business' debts. Many businesses begin as sole proprietorships and graduate to more complex business forms as the business develops.

Sole Proprietorship Taxation

As the owner of a sole proprietorship, you're taxed as an individual and you report your income on federal Form 1040, along with a special form for sole proprietors called Schedule C, Profit or Loss From Business.

Advantages and Disadvantages of the Sole Proprietorship

Advantages of the sole proprietorship:

- Owners can establish a sole proprietorship easily and inexpensively.
- Sole proprietorships carry little, if any, ongoing formalities.
- Sole proprietors need not pay unemployment tax on themselves. (Although they must pay unemployment tax on employees.)
- Owners may freely mix business and personal assets.

Disadvantages of the sole proprietorship:

- Owners are subject to unlimited personal liability for the debts, losses, and liabilities of the business.
- There is the inability to raise capital through the issuance of equity.
- Sole proprietorships rarely survive the death or incapacity of their owners, and so do not retain value.

The Partnership

A partnership is a business form created automatically when two or more persons engage in a business enterprise for profit. A partnership—in its various forms—offers its multiple owners flexibility and relative simplicity in organization and operation. In the case of limited partnerships and limited liability partnerships, a partnership can even offer a degree of liability protection.

Partnerships can be formed with a handshake, and often, they are. Responsible partners, however, will seek to have their partnership arrangement memorialized in a partnership agreement—preferably with the assistance of an attorney. The cost to have an attorney draft a partnership agreement can vary between $500 and $2,000 depending on the complexity of the partnership arrangement and the experience and location of the attorney.

Don't operate a partnership without a written partnership agreement! Because of their informality and their ease of formation, partnerships are the most likely business form to result in disputes and lawsuits between owners. Oral partnership arrangements are usually the reason.

Partnership Taxation

Technically speaking, partnerships are not taxed. Partnership income passes through the partnership without incurring tax, and is then each partner is taxed personally. Although a partnership pays no tax, it is required to disclose its earnings and distributions to the Internal Revenue Service and state tax authorities on an annual information return.

By comparison, a corporation pays tax on its earnings and each shareholder is taxed personally on distributions and dividends. The dual effect of corporate taxation is aptly referred to as double taxation. However, corporations may enjoy the benefits of partnership taxation if they elect to be taxed as a Subchapter S corporation. See below for a complete discussion of S corporations and their taxation.

Types of Partnerships

When it comes to partnerships, you can choose a simple general partnership, a limited partnership, or a limited liability partnership.

General Partnership

By default, a standard partnership is referred to as a general partnership, which is the simplest of all partnerships. An oral partnership will almost always be a general partnership. In a general partnership, all partners share in the management of the entity. Matters with respect to the ordinary business operations of the partners are decided by a majority of the partners. Of course, some partners can own a greater share of the entity than other partners, in which case, their vote counts according to their percentage ownership—much like voting of shares in a corporation. All partners, regardless of their share, are responsible for the general partnership's liabilities.

Limited Partnership

The limited partnership is more complex than a general partnership. It is a partnership owned by two classes of partners: the general partners, who manage the enterprise and are personally liable for its debts; and the limited partners, who contribute capital and share in the profits but normally do not participate in the management of the enterprise. Another notable distinction between the two classes of partners is that limited partners incur no liability for partnership debts beyond their capital contributions. Limited partners enjoy liability protection much like the shareholders of a corporation.

To establish a limited partnership, most states require a filing with their secretary of state. Some states, most notably California, allow the oral creation of a limited partnership. Of course, establishing a limited partnership with nothing more than an oral agreement is unwise because these agreements will likely lead to disputes and may not offer liability protection to limited partners.

Limited Liability Partnership

Yet another form of partnership is the limited liability partnership (LLP). An LLP is a partnership comprised of licensed professionals such as attorneys, accountants, and architects. The partners in an LLP may enjoy personal liability protection for the acts of other partners (but each partner remains liable for his own actions). State laws generally require LLPs to maintain generous insurance policies or cash reserves to pay claims brought against the LLP.

Advantages and Disadvantages of the Partnership

Advantages of the partnership:

- Owners can start partnerships relatively easily and inexpensively.
- Partnerships do not require annual meetings, and require few ongoing formalities.

Disadvantages of the partnership:

- All owners are subject to unlimited personal liability for the debts, losses, and liabilities of the business (except in the cases of limited partnerships and limited liability partnerships).

- Individual partners bear responsibility for the actions of other partners.

- Poorly organized partnerships and oral partnerships can lead to disputes among owners.

The Limited Liability Company

Another form of doing business is the limited liability company (LLC), which is often described as a hybrid business form. It combines the liability protection of a corporation with the tax treatment and ease of administration of a partnership. The LLC is a relatively new business form. There is little or no historical precedent for LLCs; they are essentially creations of the state legislatures. The great bulk of laws authorizing LLCs in the United States were passed in the 1980s and 1990s.

The limited liability company, as the name suggests, offers liability protection to its owners for company debts and liabilities.

LLCs do not have shareholders or partners, they have members. They do not have shares like a corporation; they have membership interests. They do not have articles of incorporation, they have articles of organization. (See Appendix A's Form 1 for a sample of California's articles of organization.) An LLC may be managed by its members, much like a general partnership is managed. Alternatively, an LLC may be centrally managed by one or more managers specifically appointed by the members, much like a corporation.

The LLC has been an instantly popular business form with small businesspersons. For some, it is an attractive alternative to a corporation, but the LLC has disadvantages. The limited liability company is a new business form, and courts have not yet developed a body of legal precedent governing LLCs. Thus, LLC owners and professionals may face operating questions and issues for which they have little or no legal guidance.

Furthermore, for companies that wish to pursue venture capital, and/or eventually pursue an initial public offering, the LLC is not an appropriate alternative to a corporation. Venture capitalists and angel investors shy away from investing in LLCs. The medium of exchange in the public securities markets is shares of stock in corporations, not LLCs. Of course, these disadvantages apply to partnerships as well. Lastly, the cost of setting up an LLC is roughly equivalent to setting up a corporation.

If you are interested in learning more about LLCs, consider the book, *The Essential Limited Liability Company Handbook,* by Corporate Agents, Inc. The book provides state-by-state information resources, plus clear explanations of legal and financial issues concerning LLCs. For more information, go to:

Oasis Press
http://www.oasispress.com

LLC Taxation

LLCs are almost universally taxed in the same manner as partnerships. Like partnership income, LLC income passes through the LLC tax-free and is only taxed when the LLC's owners receive the income. Although LLCs pay no tax, they are required to disclose their earnings and distributions to the Internal Revenue Service and state tax authorities on an annual information return.

Advantages and Disadvantages of the LLC

Advantages of the limited liability company:

- Limited liability companies do not require annual meetings and require few ongoing formalities.
- Owners are protected from personal liability for company debts and obligations.

Disadvantages of the limited liability company:

- Limited liability companies do not have a reliable body of legal precedent.
- They are not an appropriate vehicle for businesses seeking to eventually become public.
- They are more expensive to set-up than partnerships.
- They usually require periodic filings with the state and annual fees.

The Corporation

The term, corporation, comes from the Latin word, *corpus*, which means body. A corporation is a body—it is a legal person in the eyes of the law. It can bring lawsuits, can buy and sell property, can contract, can be taxed, and can even commit crime.

Its most notable feature? A corporation protects its owners from personal liability for corporate debts and obligations—within limits. See the section entitled "Protecting Yourself from Liability" in Chapter 3 for information on the limits of corporate liability protection.

Unlike a sole proprietorship, a corporation has perpetual life. When shareholders pass on or leave a corporation, they can transfer their shares to others who can continue a corporation's business. A corporation is owned by its shareholders, managed by its board of directors, and in most cases, operated by its officers. The shareholders elect the directors, who in turn appoint the corporate officers. In small corporations, the same person may serve in multiple roles—as shareholder, director, and officer.

If you are going to raise investment capital, then corporations are ideal. A corporation seeking to raise capital need only sell shares of its stock. The purchasing shareholders pay cash or property for their stock, and they then become part owners in the corporation. Of course, the sale of corporate stock is heavily regulated by the United States Securities and Exchange Commission, and by state securities laws.

A corporation's shareholders, directors, officers, and managers must observe particular formalities in a corporation's operation and administration. For example, decisions regarding a corporation's management must often be made by formal vote, and must be recorded in the corporate minutes. Meetings of shareholders and directors must be properly noticed, and must meet quorum requirements. Finally, corporations must meet annual reporting requirements in their state of incorporation, and in states where they do significant business. See Chapter 3 for a complete discussion of corporate formalities.

Corporate Taxation

As discussed above, partnership income passes through a partnership without incurring income tax at the partnership level. Unlike a partnership, a corporation pays income tax on its earnings. Corporations file their own federal income tax return on Form 1120. When corporations pay salaries to workers or dividends to shareholders, the workers and shareholders are taxed again. This dual effect of corporate taxation is aptly referred to as double taxation.

Double taxation sounds much worse than it is. Remember that salaries are a tax-deductible expense for a corporation. Thus, only profit is subject to double taxation. Some corporations deal with the double taxation problem by simply paying out all of the corporation's profits as salaries and bonuses.

The corporate federal income tax rate (like the individual tax rate) begins at 15 percent, and graduates to maximum 35 percent, but certain surtaxes cause tax "bubbles" at lower incomes. The table below illustrates the federal corporate income tax rates at various income levels. Note that Congress routinely adjusts income tax rates, so this table is subject to change. See the instructions to Form 1120 for current tax rates. By comparison, individual tax rates graduate to a maximum of 39.6 percent.

U.S. Federal Corporate Income Tax Rates

Income Level ($)	Effective Tax Rate (%)
0–50,000	15
50,001–75,000	25
75,001–100,000	34
100,001–335,000	39
335,001–10,000,000	34
10,000,001–15,000,000	35
15,000,001–18,333,333	38
Above 18,333,333	35

Corporations may choose a fiscal year that differs from the fiscal year of its shareholders. This creates opportunities to achieve tax savings through the deferral of income. For example, a business that receives a large increase in revenues in December can make its fiscal year end on November 30—thereby deferring the December receipts until the following fiscal year. You should seek the advice of an accountant when making decisions regarding your fiscal year.

Corporations are also taxed at the state level. The states have adopted a dizzying variety of approaches to corporate taxation. Most common is the corporate income tax. Corporate income tax rates are lower than federal rates and tend to range between 4 and 11 percent depending on the state. Not all states levy an income tax. Also common are state corporate taxes based upon assets in use in the state, and taxes based upon outstanding shares of stock.

A common theme in state corporate taxation is that a given state will only tax corporate activity that occurs within that state. This doctrine is called apportionment. For example, a state will only tax corporate income to the extent that such income flows from activities within the state.

A corporation or other business operating in several states must file a tax return with the IRS as well as all states in which it operates. Of course, each state has its own legal definition of what degree of business operation will trigger taxation.

Special Types of Corporation

As with partnerships, you can choose to form a special type of corporation, including a C corporation, close corporation, S corporation, or professional corporation. To see which one will be better for you, consider their definitions and your own goals for running your business.

C Corporation

A C corporation is little more than an ordinary corporation. So, a for-profit corporation that is not a professional corporation, and has not elected to be an S corporation is sometimes referred to as a C corporation.

Close Corporation

A close corporation is generally a smaller corporation that elects close corporation status, and is therefore entitled to operate without the strict formalities normally required in the operation of standard corporations. Many small business owners find this benefit invaluable. In essence, a close corporation is a corporation whose shareholders and directors are entitled to operate much like a partnership. The close corporation election is made at the state level, and state laws vary with respect to the eligibility of close corporation status and with respect to the rules governing them. Some states, however, do not authorize close corporations.

Corporations must meet particular requirements to be eligible for close corporation status. Generally speaking, a close corporation cannot have more than a particular number of shareholders—between 30 and 35 is the limit in most states. A close corporation cannot make a public offering of its stock. Typically, shareholders must agree unanimously to close corporation status, and a written shareholders' agreement governing the affairs of the corporation must be drafted. (Shareholders' agreements are complex documents and should be left to experienced counsel.)

Close corporations enjoy relaxed rules with respect to the formalities of governance. For example, close corporation shareholders typically do not hold formal annual meetings. Close corporation shareholders may override the directors and act on their own—thereby usurping an authority typically lodged with the directors.

Typically, the statement electing close corporation status must appear in the articles of incorporation. For example, the following clause effectively elects close corporation status in the state of California: "All of this Corporation's issued shares of all classes shall be held of record by not more than 35 persons, and this Corporation is a close corporation."

The shares in a close corporation are subject to restrictions on resale by both shareholder agreements and state law. Shareholders in close corporations have a great degree of control over other shareholders that wish to sell their shares to outsiders. Typically, close corporation shareholder agreements contain buy-sell provisions that give existing shareholders first rights of refusal with respect to subsequent sales or transfers of shares. Thereby control of close corporations remains with insiders.

Close corporations present a risk to a subsequent purchaser of shares of the corporation because a subsequent sale of a close corporation's shares often violates laws against transfer or violates the corporation's underlying shareholders' agreements. A subsequent purchaser of shares could eventually find his purchase to be void. So, most states require that a legend appear on the stock certificates advising of close corporation status. The following clause is required to be imprinted on share certificates of close corporations in California:

> "This corporation is a close corporation. The number of holders of record cannot exceed (not more than 35). Any attempted voluntary inter vivos transfer which would violate this requirement is void. Refer to the articles, bylaws and shareholder agreements on file with the secretary of the corporation for further restrictions."[1]

Because close corporation shares are subject to resale restrictions, the shares are not liquid and the value of such shares can remain significantly depressed. A present shareholder in a close corporation wishing to sell his interest must meet the stringent requirements of any shareholder's agreement. The remaining shareholders typically have rights of first refusal to purchase the shares on attractive terms. A potential buyer, if inclined to endure

---

1. Cal. Corp. Code § 418(c).

the complexities of a purchase of close corporation shares, will find his interest difficult to transfer upon becoming a shareholder. These factors all contribute to a depression in the value of shares in a close corporation. This phenomenon is called the illiquidity discount. When shares are not liquid, whether by operation of a shareholder's agreement or by other legal restriction, the value of such shares is discounted.

Close corporations are generally more expensive to organize than C corporations or S corporations because they require a written shareholders' agreement, which typically must be drafted by an attorney. However, close corporations require fewer ongoing formalities, so save time and money by electing close corporation status.

So to review, the advantages of the close corporation:

- It requires fewer formalities than a standard corporation.
- Close corporation shareholders have a greater degree of control over sales of shares to outsiders.

Disadvantages of the close corporation:

- Close corporations are not available in all states.
- Shareholders have increased responsibilities and participation.
- Close corporation shares have limited resale value.
- A close corporation cannot make a public offering of its stock.

S Corporation

Subchapter S of the Internal Revenue Code permits eligible smaller corporations to avoid double taxation and be taxed as partnerships. Corporations must elect Subchapter S status by filing Internal Revenue Service Form 2553. You will find a blank Form 2553 near the end of Appendix A. Corporations that make such an election are known as S corporations. An S corporation differs from a standard C corporation solely with respect to its taxation.

A corporation must meet certain conditions to be eligible for a Subchapter S election. First, it must have no more than 75 shareholders. In calculating the 75 shareholder limit, a husband and wife count as one shareholder. Also, only the following entities may be shareholders: individuals, estates, certain trusts, certain partnerships, tax-exempt charitable organizations, and other S corporations (but only if the other S corporation is the sole shareholder).

S corporations may only have one class of stock. A corporation must make the Subchapter S election no later than two months and 15 days after the first day of the taxable year—it cannot wait until the end of the taxable year to elect. Subchapter S election requires the consent of all shareholders.

The states treat S corporations differently. Some states disregard Subchapter S status entirely, offering no tax break at all. Other states honor the federal election automatically. Finally, some states require the filing of a state-specific form to complete Subchapter S election. The State Reference Tables in Appendix B outline each state's Subchapter S treatment.

An S corporation may revoke its Subchapter S status by either failing to meet the conditions of eligibility for S corporations, or by filing with the IRS no later than two months and 15 days after the first day of the taxable year. Once the revocation becomes effective, the corporation will be taxed as a corporation.

Professional Corporation

Professional corporations are organized and operated solely by licensed professionals such as attorneys, accountants, and architects. The shareholders in a professional corporation may enjoy personal liability protection for the acts of other shareholders (but all shareholders remain liable for their own professional misconduct). State laws generally require professional corporations to maintain generous insurance policies or cash reserves to pay claims brought against the corporation. Professional corporations are more sophisticated enterprises than regular corporations, and their organization should be left to a qualified attorney.

Advantages and Disadvantages of Incorporation

Advantages of the corporation:

- Owners are protected from personal liability for company debts and obligations.
- Corporations have a reliable body of legal precedent to guide owners and managers.
- Corporations are the best vehicle for eventual public companies.
- Corporations can more easily raise capital through the sale of securities.
- Corporations can easily transfer ownership through the transfer of securities.
- Corporations can have an unlimited life.
- Corporations enjoy tax benefits.

Disadvantages of the corporation:

- Corporations require annual meetings and require owners and directors to observe certain formalities.
- They are more expensive to set-up than partnerships and sole proprietorships.
- They require periodic filings with the state and annual fees.

See the Business Form Comparison Table on the following page to get a review of each business organization's pros and cons.

Business Form Comparison Table

	Corporation	LLC	Partnership	Sole Prop
Ease of set-up	More difficult	More difficult	Less difficult	Easy
Initial filing fees, state fees, and legal fees	High	High	Medium	Low
Owners are personally protected from liability for the organization's debts	Yes	Yes	No (except in limited partnerships)	No
Entity must make annual or biennial state filings	Yes	Yes	Almost never	No
Entity must pay annual or biennial state fees	Yes	Yes	Almost never	No
Requires formalities and annual meetings	Yes (except close corp)	No	No	No
Can exist indefinitely	Yes	Yes	No	No
Can issue shares or interest in exchange for cash	Yes	Yes	Yes	No
Appropriate entity to raise venture capital	Yes	No	No	No
Appropriate entity to become publicly traded	Yes	No	No	No
Entity can elect to be taxed as a corporation	Yes	No	No	No
Entity can elect to be taxed as partnership	Yes	Yes	Yes	No
Can choose fiscal year other than that of its owners	Yes	No	No	No

Chapter 2

The Twelve Steps to Incorporation

Self-incorporation can seem daunting, but the task is actually a series of small, simple tasks. At the end of this chapter, complete the Incorporation Worksheet to help you organize these tasks. The State Reference Tables in Appendix B offer contact information and resources for all 50 states and the District of Columbia. Appendix A also offers dozens of model documents to assist you.

Who Plays a Role?

Before learning the twelve steps to incorporating, you need to know who plays what role in the incorporation process. There are basically five major players, including the incorporator, the shareholders, the directors, the officers, and the secretary of state's office.

The Incorporator's Role

An incorporator is the person or entity that organizes a corporation and files its articles of incorporation. The incorporator enjoys certain powers, such as he can take corporate actions before directors and officers are appointed. For example, an incorporator can amend articles of incorporation, approve bylaws, and appoint directors. Typically, an incorporator's power is quite broad. "If the persons who are to serve as directors ... have not been named in the certificate of incorporation, the incorporator or incorporators ... shall manage the affairs of the corporation and may do whatever is necessary and proper to perfect the organization of the corporation."[2]

Once the incorporator forms the corporation and appoints its directors, the directors then assume the management of the corporation, and the incorporator's role ceases. When an attorney forms a corporation on behalf of a client, the attorney serves as incorporator. If you intend to use this book to guide you with your incorporation, you will be serving as the incorporator.

The Shareholders' Role

Shareholders are the owners of a corporation. Shareholders' rights and duties are defined by state law, the articles of incorporation, the bylaws, and a shareholders' agreement, if any. Except in the case of a close corporation, shareholders do not actively participate in the management of a corporation. Shareholders delegate the corporation's management to the corporation's directors. Shareholders elect directors at annual meetings, but can also remove and replace directors at special meetings called at any time.

The Directors' Role

Directors are the elected managers of a corporation. Directors enjoy broad powers, but typically delegate a corporation's day-to-day responsibilities to corporate officers. Directors can be, but need not be, shareholders. Generally, directors guide policy and make major decisions regarding corporate affairs, but do not represent the corporation when dealing with vendors and customers. Bear in mind that the same person may serve as both director and officer. The directors are collectively known as the board of directors, and the elected head of the board is the chairman of the board. Tasks typically within the gambit of the directors' authority include:

- Electing officers;
- Issuing shares of corporate stock;
- Voting on acquisitions and mergers;
- Approving loans to the corporation;
- Approving stock option plans; and
- Approving large purchases of real estate and capital equipment.

---

2. Del. Gen. Corp. Law § 107.

The Officers' Role

Officers operate a corporation on a day-to-day basis. They are formally appointed by directors at either annual or special meetings of the board of directors. Corporations typically have a president/chief executive officer (CEO), a treasurer/chief financial officer (CFO), and a secretary. Vice presidents are optional.

The president/CEO is a corporation's senior manager, and typically stands at the top of a corporation's management hierarchy. The treasurer often also serves as the CFO, and has primary responsibility for managing the corporation's financial affairs. Such duties include recordkeeping, overseeing bookkeeping, reporting on the corporation's financial condition, and preparing financial information for tax reporting. The corporation's secretary maintains the corporate records. Because the corporate secretary's role is not particularly demanding, the secretary often serves in some other position within the corporation as well.

Small corporations often have very few shareholders and managers. So, it is not uncommon that a corporation has one person who is the sole shareholder, sole director, and CEO. Prudence dictates that a corporation have at least a second person to serve as secretary because this officer is charged with witnessing the signature of the CEO.

Tasks typically within the scope of an officer's authority include:

- Managing the corporation on a day-to-day basis;
- Hiring and firing employees;
- Negotiating and singing contracts;
- Dealing with customers and vendors; and
- Maintaining the corporation's records.

The Secretary of State's Role

A secretary of state is a state official charged with responsibility for receiving and archiving legal documents, including corporation papers. Your state, however, may have an equivalent department with a different name, such as Hawaii's Department of Commerce and Consumer Affairs or Arizona's Corporation Commission. Regardless of the name, each state's corporate filing office operates much the same.

Your corporation's most foundational document is its articles of incorporation, and you file your articles with the secretary of state to begin the life of your corporation. But the secretary of state's role does not end there. The secretary of state is also the department that receives corporations' annual reports and maintains records on all corporations. If a corporation fails to pay its taxes or fails to file its periodic reports, the secretary of state may withdraw a corporation's "good standing" status. Corporations do not file their bylaws or their minutes with the secretary of state.

If a corporation becomes seriously delinquent in its tax and reporting responsibilities, the secretary of state may eventually order a corporation's administrative dissolution. An administrative dissolution is one manner in which a corporation may conclude its otherwise perpetual life. Each state has different rules for what constitutes a delinquency serious enough to warrant an administrative dissolution. Both dissolution and the withdrawal of good standing status can lead to a failure of a corporation's liability protection. See Chapter 3 for further information on maintaining good standing with the secretary of state.

Step 1: Where Should You Incorporate?

Your corporation's life begins when you file articles of incorporation with the secretary of state or its equivalent. Several factors shall guide your decision of which state is the best for your incorporation. Those factors include:

- The state or states in which your business operates;
- State taxation;
- Initial corporate filing fees;
- Annual filing fees and annual reporting requirements; and
- State-specific advantages, such as privacy rights and directors' rights.

As a general rule, if your business is small and operates and sells only in one state, then you should incorporate in your state of operation. States generally require out-of-state (foreign) corporations to register and pay fees in the corporation's state of operation. For example, a Delaware corporation that transacts business in California must register in California as a foreign corporation,[3] and must pay a filing fee and annual minimum franchise tax. Registration in a foreign state is often called qualification. Thus, the benefits of incorporating out of state are limited by such foreign registration rules.

---

3. Cal. Corp. Code § 2105.

If, however, your business operates in several states or if you expect to expand nationally, then you should consider incorporation in the state that is most favorable for you. Traditionally, the most popular state for incorporation has been Delaware. Delaware is corporation-friendly and offers low corporate taxation. Thereby, the state of Delaware traditionally enjoyed an abundant stream of registration fees, and a sizeable industry developed to serve the corporations that filed there. Eventually, other states grew wise and mirrored Delaware's corporation-friendly approach. A notable example is Nevada, which has recently emerged with an aggressive program to attract companies to incorporate there. Despite this competition, Delaware still offers many advantages.

Advantages of Delaware Incorporation

Delaware incorporation carries many benefits, among which are the following:

- Delaware annual corporate franchise tax is inexpensive.
- Delaware law permits corporations to liberally shield directors from personal liability resulting from their actions as directors.
- Delaware has a separate court system, the Court of Chancery that specifically litigates corporate matters. The Court of Chancery is widely respected and has developed a sophisticated body of corporate law.
- Delaware permits corporations to operate with a great degree of anonymity.
- No minimum capital investment is required to form a Delaware Corporation.
- The Delaware Division of Corporations provides excellent customer service.
- Delaware incorporation offers some degree of prestige.

Advantages of Nevada Incorporation

Nevada incorporation carries many benefits, among which are the following:

- Nevada has low corporate taxes: no corporate income tax, no taxes on corporate shares, and no franchise tax. Nevada corporate taxes are lower than Delaware corporate taxes.
- Nevada law permits corporations to liberally shield directors and officers from personal liability resulting from lawful corporate duties.
- Nevada permits corporations to operate with a great degree of anonymity and privacy.

- Nevada has no information sharing agreement with the Internal Revenue Service.
- The Nevada secretary of state provides excellent customer service.

You should also consider the initial cost of incorporation, as well as periodic filing fees and period reporting requirements. See Appendix B for information on state filing fees and periodic reporting requirements.

Step 2: Select Your Corporate Name

At this stage in the incorporation process, you must choose your corporate name. Understand, of course, that you may use a trade name in the public marketplace other than your corporate name. This is called "doing business as" (DBA) a fictitious name. For example, your company could operate a store under the trade name "Evolution," but the corporation name could be Evolution Water Company, Inc., or could be any other name for that matter. You will find more on DBA requirements later in this discussion.

The single greatest consideration when choosing a name is ensuring that no other person or entity is currently using the name. This consideration is guided by two factors. First, your use of a company name may infringe on the trademark or service mark rights of others. Infringing on the trademark rights of other may result in legal complications. Second, the secretary of state's office will not register a new corporation with the same name as an existing corporation.

Thus, you may wish to search for existing trademarks and corporate names to ensure that your desired name is available.

Searching for Existing Trademarks

Begin by performing a trademark search. You can hire a professional service to perform a trademark search for you. This service can range between $300 and $1,200. The value of such professional search services, however, has been eclipsed by free services on the Internet.

You can search registered and pending trademarks at:

U.S. Patent and Trademark Office
http://www.uspto.gov/web/menu/tm.html

Once you are at the website, use the Trademark Electronic Search System (TESS), and then use the New User Form Search. At the search window, enter the name that you wish to use in the box entitled "Search Term." Make sure the "Field" term is set to "Combined Word Mark." To ensure that your search effectively locates all potential conflicts, be sure to do the following:

- Search for phonetic variants of your proposed name, because phonetically similar marks can cause a trademark conflict. For example, if your company name is Cybertech, search for Cybertek, Cybertex, Sybertex, etc.
- Search for both the plural and singular versions of your proposed name.
- If your name uses more than one word, search for each word individually.
- Follow the instructions in the use of wildcard search terms.

Searching for trademarks, though, is an imperfect science, and no search can be expected to discover all potential users of a mark. Remember that trademark rights are created by the use of a mark, and not by registration. Thus, unregistered marks may be valid marks—and they are much more difficult to discover. The last step of your trademark conflict search should be an Internet search with one of the popular search engines. Such a search will likely discover any existing users of your proposed name.

Searching for Existing Corporate Names

Assuming that your name does not trigger a conflict with a registered or unregistered trademark, you should then search an online database of existing corporate names with the secretary of state in the state in which you intend to incorporate. Nearly all secretary of state websites offer free searching of existing corporate names. See Appendix B for information on locating the secretary of state's website in your state of incorporation. Alternatively, some secretary of states' offices offer informal searches over the telephone, but searching a database is always preferred.

Your corporation's name should reflect corporate status. Most states require a corporate identifier. Perhaps more importantly, you should always hold yourself out to the public as a corporation to ensure maximum liability protection. Therefore your corporation's name should include one of the following terms:

- Corporation or Corp.
- Incorporated or Inc.
- Some states allow "Limited:" or "Ltd.", but this designation may imply a limited partnership or limited liability company.

Your corporation's name should NOT include any of the following terms, which are usually restricted by state and/or federal law, unless your corporation meets the legal requirements for such terms:

- Bank
- Trust or Trustee
- Insurance
- Investment and loan
- Thrift
- Doctor
- Mortgage
- Cooperative
- Olympic or Olympiad

Reserving Your Corporate Name

When you have selected an appropriate name, you may wish to reserve the name of the corporation. This step is optional. Nearly all states offer a name reservation service. Typically, the service requires you to file a brief name reservation application with the secretary of state's office. Appendix B features information on name reservation in particular states, appropriate forms, and associated filing fees.

Step 3: Select the Type of Corporation

As discussed in Chapter 1, there are several variations of the standard for-profit corporation. Specifically, such variants are close corporation, S corporation, and professional corporation. The S corporation election is made after the filing of the articles of incorporation, but the decision to elect Subchapter S status is usually made during the planning stage. Alternatively, close corporation status and professional corporation status must be declared within the articles of incorporation. Thus, this decision must be made early in your planning. Recall, however, that close corporation status is not available in all states.

Step 4: Select the Registered Agent

A registered agent is a person or entity that is authorized and obligated to receive legal papers on behalf of a corporation. The registered agent is identified in the articles of incorporation, but can typically be changed upon the filing of a notice with the secretary of state. The registered agent serves an important function: a corporation is not a physical person so without such a designated representative, service of legal papers on a corporation would be impossible. The registered agent is designated in the articles of incorporation by language such as, "The name and address in the State of California of this Corporation's initial agent for service of process is John Jones, 123 Elm Street, San Francisco, California 94107."

Keep in mind that your state of incorporation may use a different term than registered agent. Typical equivalents include agent for service of process and local agent.

The agent can be you, a family member, a corporate officer, an attorney, or a company that specializes in corporation services. Keep in mind that the registered agent's name is a public record; if you desire anonymity, then hire a professional to perform this service. The agent must have a physical address in the state of incorporation. Thus, if your business does not operate in the state of incorporation, you will need to hire a registered agent in the state of incorporation. You must consider this additional expense when incorporating out of state. Such services typically range from $50 to $150 per year. If you wish to hire a local agent, you may do so by following the link to Business Filings at the following website:

LearnAboutLaw.com
http://www.learnaboutlaw.com

Follow the link for Business Filings, Inc. This company offers resident agent services in all 50 states at reasonable prices.

Having an attorney or professional firm to serve as agent has advantages. Because the primary role of an agent is to receive service of legal papers, an attorney or professional firm is likely to maintain a consistent address and is likely to understand the nature of any legal papers served upon them. The agent will also receive important state and federal mail such as tax forms, annual corporate report forms, legal notices and the like.

The secretary of state's office where you file your corporation will most likely not check to see if you have properly secured the services of a registered agent. If you do not select a registered agent properly, the secretary of state will blindly mail you documents at the registered agent's address, and you will not receive them. Thus, you should hire your registered agent either before or concurrently with the filing of your articles of incorporation. Form 6 in Appendix A is a sample letter suitable to hire a registered agent.

Step 5: Decide Who Will Incorporate

At this stage in your incorporation, you must decide whether you will file and organize your corporation on your own or hire a discount incorporation service or an attorney. Each approach has its advantages and disadvantages.

Self-Incorporation

Obviously, the greatest benefit of self-incorporation is initial savings. Self-incorporation carries the lowest initial cost. Of course, as with any legal matter, cutting costs can often cost more later. For example, if your corporation is not properly organized, ambitious creditors may later reach your personal assets by piercing the corporate veil. See Appendix C for a definition of piercing the corporate veil.

Discount Incorporation Services

A slightly more expensive alternative is to hire a discount incorporation service. Such services range from $200 to $300 per incorporation and offer a streamlined but competent service. Of course, such services are essentially filing services, and include only the following:

- Filing of articles of incorporation with the appropriate state office;
- Selection of close corporation status;
- Preparation of boilerplate bylaws; and
- Preparation of boilerplate minutes of organizational meeting of directors.

Such services generally do not include post-filing steps, such as the following which you must accomplish on your own:

- Review and revision of bylaws, if necessary;
- Review and revision of minutes for organizational meeting of directors, if necessary;
- Conducting the organizational meeting of directors;

- Issuing stock;
- Avoiding complications with state securities laws;
- Filing initial corporate reports; and
- Filing periodic reports.

Discount incorporation services do offer value. They can often navigate the bureaucratic complexities of various states, and can provide prompt service and tested documents. However, although discount incorporation services do provide boilerplate bylaws and proposed minutes of organizational meeting, such documents often contain fill-in-the-blank and optional provisions that can baffle an inexperienced incorporator.

Business Filings, Inc. offers competent incorporation and LLC services at reasonable prices. They also offer online filing, online customer service, a free online name availability check, although name reservation services are not free. Business Filings, Inc. can incorporate your business in any state, and the fees range from $75 for a basic service to $295 for a comprehensive service. For more information, contact:

Business Filings, Inc.
(800) 981-7183
http://www.learnaboutlaw.com

Hiring an Experienced Business Attorney

Finally, you may wish to hire a business attorney to incorporate your business for you.

A qualified business attorney can do the following:

- Suggest alternatives and solutions that would not occur to even the most diligent layperson;
- Assist with more complex features of business organizations, such as close corporations and shareholder agreements;
- Anticipate problems before they arise;
- Prepare bylaws and minutes of the organizational meeting of directors according to your specific needs; and
- Ensure that no federal or state securities laws are violated.

How to find a qualified business attorney:

- Recommendations from friends and associates usually yield excellent matches between attorney and businessperson.

- Local bar associations in major metropolitan areas usually operate referral services. They pre-screen attorneys, so you can be assured of the attorney's experience.

- State bar associations now commonly maintain on-line records of attorney discipline—avoid attorneys with a history of discipline problems.

What you can expect to pay: The hourly rate for business attorneys ranges from $100 to $350 per hour. The lower end of the scale will apply outside of major metropolitan areas and for less experienced attorneys. Business attorneys often charge a flat fee for services such as forming LLCs and corporations. You can expect to pay between $500 to $2,000 for complete incorporation services.

Step 6: Determine the Stock Structure

Your corporation will issue shares of stock to its owners as part of the organization process. Shares of stock represent the ownership of the corporation. Shares in a corporation are broadly referred to as equity. You must choose your stock structure early in the incorporation process because you must set forth the stock structure in the articles of incorporation.

All corporations must have at least one class of stock with voting rights. Without at least one class of voting stock, a corporation's shareholders could not elect directors—and therefore the corporation would be powerless to take any legal action. Most corporations, especially small corporations, have only one class of stock. This type of stock is called voting common stock.

Corporations may have one or more additional classes of stock. Secondary classes of voting stock appear in infinite varieties. However, classes of stock can be broadly categorized into three groups: common, preferred, and hybrid. Common stock is simply plain voting stock.

Preferred stock is stock that entitles its holder to a monetary priority or preference over another class of shares. Typically, preferred stock entitles the holder to priority of receipt of dividends and asset distributions upon the corporation's liquidation. In other words, preferred stockholders get paid first, and common stockholders get what remains. Preferred stock often carries no voting rights. Sometimes, preferred stock is convertible into common stock.

Hybrid stock refers to debt instruments which are convertible into stock—they are not true equity instruments. For example, a promissory note—a document evidencing a loan—that is convertible into shares of common stock, is hybrid stock.

The rights and privileges of all a corporation's classes of stock must be set forth in the articles of incorporation with a certain degree of particularity. Sample clauses establishing multiple classes of shares appear in Appendix A.

An important concept in understanding share structure is the distinction between authorized shares and outstanding or issued shares. Authorized shares are shares of a corporation's stock that its directors have the legal authority to issue. The number of authorized shares is stated in a corporation's articles of incorporation. A corporation can never issue shares beyond the number of authorized shares—or the excess shares have no legal effect. Outstanding or issued shares are a corporation's shares that have issued to shareholders by its directors. Thus, authorized shares are like blank checks in a checkbook; they have no legal effect until formally issued by a vote of directors. A corporation's directors create shares of stock by voting to issue shares to shareholders. Once issued, the shares represent the legal ownership of the corporation. When the directors vote to issue shares, typically a corporate officer will print a share certificate showing the issue date, number of shares issued, and name of the party to whom the shares are issued.

Some states charge a filing fee for articles of incorporation based upon a corporation's authorized shares—higher amounts of authorized shares will trigger a higher fee.

The number of authorized shares will dictate how many shares your corporation may issue, and for what price your corporation may offer them. Some corporations authorize and issue just one share of stock to a single shareholder, and some authorize and issue trillions of shares. More typically, smaller corporations authorize between 1,000 and one million shares. Corporations with lofty expectations of tremendous growth will authorize enormous numbers of shares from one million to 100 million. A high number of authorized shares ensures that a single share of stock will not command too high a price. Ideally, a single share of stock offered to the professional capital community should be less than $2 per share, even less in the very early stages of a company's development.

When determining the amount of shares to authorize in the articles, you must also consider if your state charges a filing fee based upon the number of authorized shares. If necessary, keep the number of authorized shares low enough to keep the filing fee as inexpensive as possible.

Step 7: File the Articles of Incorporation

The life of a corporation begins with the preparation and filing of articles of incorporation. Typically a one-page document, the articles of incorporation sets out the following basic information:

- The name of the corporation;
- The name and address of the registered agent or "agent for service of process," the person or entity that is authorized to receive legal papers on behalf of a corporation;
- The amount and type of stock that the corporation is authorized to issue;
- A statement of the corporation's purpose;
- Optionally, the names of initial directors; and
- Other optional matters, such as the election to be a close corporation.

To begin the life of a corporation, you file articles of incorporation with the secretary of state (or other equivalent department) in the state of incorporation. You must file articles of incorporation along with a filing fee, which differs in each state. You can usually pick your exact date of incorporation. If you would like a special date of incorporation for your business, such as January 1, or a birthday, contact the secretary of state's office in the state in which you intend to incorporate. Almost all states will let you designate a special date of incorporation when you file.

As a general rule, don't appoint initial directors in your articles of incorporation. Directors can easily be appointed immediately after filing by the incorporator. Articles of incorporation are public documents, so always strive to operate your corporation as discretely as possible.

You will find sample articles of incorporation for Delaware and California in Appendix A. These sample articles should be used in these states only. Fortunately, nearly every secretary of state's website offers sample articles of incorporation in either word processor or portable document format (PDF). Appendix B features the secretary of state's office (or its equivalent) for all 50 states, plus the District of Columbia.

Step 8: Order Your Corporate Kit

A corporate kit is little more than a binder where you maintain corporate records such as articles of incorporation, bylaws, minutes of meetings, and a stock ledger. Corporate kits range in price from $50 to $100. Corporate kits usually include the following:

- Model bylaws and minutes of the organizational meeting, with optional provisions;
- Blank stock certificates;
- A corporate seal; and
- A blank stock transfer ledger.

Corporate kits are available from corporation supply companies and from some office supply stores. You can obtain an inexpensive corporate kit by following the link to Business Filings at the following website:

LearnAboutLaw.com
http://www.learnaboutlaw.com

Sample Minutes and Bylaws

Corporate kits usually include sample bylaws and minutes of the corporation's organizational meeting. Bylaws are the internal operating rules of a corporation. See the section below entitled, Step 9: Prepare Corporation Bylaws, for a complete description of bylaws. The organizational meeting is a corporation's initial meeting. See Step 11: The Directors' Organizational Meeting for a complete description of a corporation's organizational meeting.

The Corporate Seal

A corporate seal is a hand-operated embossing seal that contains the name of your corporation, state of incorporation, and date of incorporation. Corporate seals are no longer required in every state, but they remain standard features in almost any corporate kit.

Stock Certificates

A stock certificate is a printed document that evidences ownership of shares in a corporation. Corporate kits include blank stock certificates. You print the certificates by running them through a printer, typing them, or filling them out by hand.

Stock Transfer Ledger

A stock transfer ledger is simply a written list of who holds a corporation's shares of stock. The transfer ledger also records sales and transfers of a corporation's shares. Responsibility for maintaining the ledger usually rests with the corporation's secretary.

Step 9: Prepare Corporation Bylaws

Bylaws are the internal operating rules of a corporation. Bylaws govern such matters as holding meetings, voting, quorums, elections, and the powers of directors and officers. Bylaws are usually set out in a five- to twenty-page document. Sample bylaws suitable for use in any state appear in Appendix A, Form 8. Your corporate kit will likely contain sample bylaws that will be more appropriately tailored to your particular state. Bylaws are not filed with the state like articles of incorporation. Instead, bylaws remain with the corporate books and records.

Your bylaws will cover the following matters:

- The powers and duties of directors and officers;
- The date and time of annual meetings of shareholders and directors;
- Procedures for the election of directors;
- Procedures for the appointment of officers;
- Procedures for the removal of directors;
- Quorum requirements for shareholder votes;
- Quorum requirements for director votes;
- Procedures for voting by written consent without appearing at a formal meeting; and
- Procedures for giving proxy to other shareholders.

Your next step is to formally adopt the bylaws on behalf of a corporation. Directors have the power to approve and adopt bylaws. Because your corporation will not yet have directors, the incorporator is empowered to approve bylaws. See Form 7 in Appendix A for a sample resolution to adopt your corporate bylaws.

Step 10: Select the Corporation's Directors

As discussed in the beginning of this chapter, directors are the elected managers of a corporation. Directors are elected by shareholders at annual meetings, and typically serve a one-year term. At subsequent annual meetings, directors are often reelected to serve for additional terms. Corporations must have at least one director.

You must first decide the number of directors that will serve in your corporation. Except for very small corporations, the most suitable number will be three directors. Some states, such as California, do not allow a corporation to have one director unless the corporation has only one shareholder.[4] Single director corporations are allowed in Delaware[5] and in Nevada,[6] and may be appropriate for small corporations. Two directors may also be suitable, but if the directors disagree on a policy decision and cannot resolve the conflict, it may lead to deadlock which may require resolution in court. Corporations with only one director may have difficulty attracting investment.

Shareholders of single director corporations are more subject to personal liability risks. Alter ego liability, which is discussed in Chapter 3, can attach to shareholders of corporations that commingle personal and corporate assets or do not observe corporate formalities. A sole director with boundless authority is more likely to disregard important formalities. Conversely, a multi-member board is more likely to reach decisions through discussion, consensus, and vote.

Directors should always avoid conflicts of interest and abstain from votes in which they have a personal interest. For example, it is improper for a director to vote on a corporation's purchase of a piece of property if the director has an ownership interest in the property. A corporation's sole director cannot abstain from such a vote, because without at least one director, a board cannot act.

Shareholders often serve as both directors and officers, especially in small corporations. You should consider the use of one or more independent directors. Independent, "outside" directors who are neither shareholders nor regular employees can bring an objective perspective to your corporation. You may also benefit from the outside director's knowledge and experience.

---

4. Cal. Corp. Code § 212.
5. Del. Gen. Corp. Law § 141(b).
6. Nev. Rev. Stat. § 78.115.

Once you have decided who will serve on the board of directors, you must formally elect your initial directors. Your newly formed corporation will not yet have shareholders, so the incorporator is empowered to elect the initial directors. See Form 7 in Appendix A for a sample to accomplish the election.

Director Liability and the Business Judgment Rule

Bear in mind that directors can be held liable for mismanagement of corporations for which they serve. Courts recognize, however, that in a competitive business environment, directors must be given wide latitude in fulfilling their duties. Thus, courts are reluctant to second-guess a director's management decision. This rule is termed the "Business Judgment Rule." It states that courts will not review directors' business decisions, or hold directors liable for errors or mistakes in judgment, so long as the directors were:

- Disinterested and independent;
- Acting in good faith; and
- Reasonably diligent in informing themselves of the facts.

Some outside directors, especially experienced professionals, will only serve on a board if the corporation provides director's and officer's liability insurance. Director's and officer's (D&O) insurance protects a corporation's appointed managers from lawsuits brought by disgruntled shareholders or aggressive corporate creditors. Such insurance, however, can be quite expensive for small corporations.

Step 11: The Directors' Organizational Meeting

To finalize your incorporation, you must have an organizational meeting of the board of directors and prepare minutes of this meeting. Because the format of the meeting is relatively standard, the minutes are nearly always drafted beforehand, and followed like a script. See Form 9, Minutes of Organizational Meeting of the Board of Directors Sample, in Appendix A.

The organizational meeting can be, but need not be, held at the corporation's principal office. A quorum of directors is required to appear at the meeting, but ideally, all initial directors should be present. The minutes documenting the meeting should record all the following matters:

- The date, time, and place of the meeting;
- The date that the articles of incorporation were filed with the secretary of state;

- The persons present at the meeting; and
- The shares are issued without any advertising and within federal and state securities exemptions.

The organizational meeting addresses the following matters:

- One person must serve as the chairman of the meeting, and another must serve as the secretary of the meeting.
- As a formality, directors should waive formal written notice of the meeting.
- The initial agent for service of process, registered agent, or resident agent designated in the articles should be confirmed in that capacity.
- The corporate seal should be approved.
- The form of stock certificates should be approved.
- The corporation's principal office should be designated.
- The officers should be appointed. Typically, officers serve without compensation, although officers often receive wages in connection with other duties in connection with the business' day-to-day operation.
- The corporation's fiscal year should be declared.
- Share of stock should be issued, and the amount and type of consideration paid for such shares should be described.
- The corporation should declare whether or not it shall elect Subchapter S status.

Step 12: Federal Tax Identification Number

Because your corporation is a legal entity, federal law requires that you obtain a Federal Employer Identification Number (EIN or FEIN). Most banks will require you to give an EIN before opening a bank account. You obtain your EIN by filling out Form SS-4, Application for Employer Identification Number, and either mailing or faxing the form to the Internal Revenue Service. If you mail the form, expect to wait up to six weeks to receive your EIN. If you fax your form to a service center, you will receive your EIN in about five days. You can also obtain an EIN immediately by calling an IRS service center during business hours. Form SS-4 appears in Appendix A, but you can also obtain a PDF file from:

Internal Revenue Service
http://www.irs.gov

To obtain your SS-4 immediately, do the following:

- Either print the form from Appendix A or download the form from the IRS' website.

- Follow the form's instructions and fill in the form's first page.

- If you wish to obtain an EIN immediately, find your state of incorporation in the section of Form SS-4 entitled "Where to Apply" on pages 2 and 3. There will be a phone number for the IRS service center that handles your region. You must have the form filled out before you call, or the representative will ask you to call back. (The IRS service centers are always busy, so be prepared to get a busy signal or wait on hold, and some IRS service centers do not provide telephone service.)

- When you reach a representative, he will ask you to recite the information on the form. The representative will enter the information directly into the IRS's computer system. The call will take about ten minutes.

- The representative will then issue to you an EIN, and a telephone number to which you must fax your completed form.

Chapter 3 outlines in detail how to observe corporate formalities and maintain your corporation in good standing once you've completed these twelve steps of incorporation.

Incorporation Worksheet

1. Proposed name of corporation: _____

   a. Trademark search for name has been completed: _____

   b. Secretary of state's office search for name has been completed: _____

2. Address of principal office: _____

3. State of incorporation: _____

4. Will the corporation be a close corporation? ☐ Yes   ☐ No

5. Corporate purpose: ☐ General   ☐ Professional practice

6. Incorporator name and address:

   _____

   _____

7. The number of directors will be designated:

   ☐ In the articles of incorporation

   ☐ In the bylaws (the sample documents provided with this volume designate the number of directors in the bylaws)

8. The number of directors that will be authorized: _____

9. Names and addresses of directors:

   _____

   _____

10. Name and address of registered agent/local agent/agent for service of process:

    _____

    _____

11. Names and addresses of initial officers:

    a. Chief Executive Officer/President:

       _____

       _____

    b. Treasurer/Chief Financial Officer:

       _____

       _____

    c. Secretary:

       _____

       _____

    d. Vice President(s) (optional):

       _____

       _____

Incorporation Worksheet (continued)

12. Authorized number of shares of common stock: _____

13. Authorized number of shares of preferred stock or secondary class of stock (optional): _____

14. Rights and privileges of preferred or secondary class of stock:

    a. Dividend priority: _____

    b. Redemption rights: _____

    c. Liquidation preference: _____

    d. Conversion rights: _____

    e. Voting rights: _____

    f. Other: _____

15. Shareholders:

Name	Address	Number and class of shares of stock	Type and amount of consideration to be paid

16. Will the corporation have a shareholder's agreement? (optional) ☐ Yes ☐ No

17. Corporation's fiscal year: _____

18. Date and time of annual shareholder's meeting: _____

19. Date and times of annual meeting of directors: _____

20. Will the corporation be an S corporation? ☐ Yes ☐ No

Operating Your Corporation

The incorporation of your company is now complete, but operating your corporation and observing corporate formalities and maintaining good standing with the secretary of state's office is an ongoing task, one that lasts throughout the life of your corporation. By maintaining your corporation in good standing, you protect yourself from liability and preserve the inherent value of your business. This chapter outlines and discusses reasons for maintaining good standing and how to go about it in the right way.

Protecting Yourself from Liability

The most notable feature of a corporation is that a corporation's shareholders are protected from personal liability for the corporation's debts and obligations.

However, liability protection for shareholders of corporations is not absolute! The doctrines of "alter ego liability," and "piercing the corporate veil" give courts the power to disregard the corporate liability shield and impose liability on shareholders in extraordinary cases of shareholder misconduct.

In the following cases of shareholder misuse of the corporation form, it is said that the shareholder is merely the corporation's alter ego, and personal liability may attach:

- Shareholders do not respect a corporation's separate identity.
- Shareholders commingle personal and corporation funds.
- Shareholders treat corporate assets as their own.
- Shareholders fail to complete or honor corporate organizational and periodic formalities.

A corporation that is not in good standing or has been dissolved can undermine the corporation's ability to shield its owners from liability. A corporation is in good standing when it is in full compliance with the law, its taxes are paid, and all periodic reports have been timely filed. A corporation can be subject to an administrative dissolution if its taxes are not paid, and its periodic filings are not made on time. A dissolution is the end of a corporation's life. In addition, the following oversights by management can threaten a corporation's ability to shield its owners from liability:

- Directors and managers fail to pay corporate and franchise taxes in the state of incorporation.
- Directors and managers fail to file annual and periodic reports in the state of incorporation.
- Directors and managers fail to notify the secretary of state of a change of address.
- Directors and managers fail to pay the annual fees of the resident agent, or fail to advise the resident agent of a change of address.

Tips for Protecting the Corporate Veil

To maintain liability protection for you and other shareholders, strictly abide by the following procedures:

- Always hold yourself out as a corporation—not as an individual. Sign documents in your capacity as a representative of the corporation, not personally, i.e., John Jones, President, SuperCorp, Inc. You should always endeavor to prevent a creditor from arguing that you personally guaranteed an obligation. Identify your corporation in advertisements, correspondence, invoices, statements, business cards, your website, etc.
- Follow your own bylaws. A crafty creditor's attorney can have an easy time asserting alter ego liability if you do not follow your own corporation's written procedures.

- Keep proper corporate records. When directors and shareholders meet, be sure to prepare minutes of the meetings. If the directors reach a decision, even informally, commit that decision to writing in the form of a written consent. Creditors wishing to pierce the corporate veil will always seek to discover improper recordkeeping.

- Obtain and maintain a corporate checking account. Furthermore, always keep your personal assets and corporate assets separate. Also, if you operate more than one corporation, keep each corporation's assets separate.

- Always keep your corporation in good standing with the secretary of state. A corporation is subject to administrative dissolution if it fails to meet its ongoing responsibilities. This means that you must always file all tax returns, including franchise tax returns, and file all periodic reporting forms. To help ensure this, maintain close contact with your registered agent and always pay him on time.

- Never dissolve a corporation that has debts outstanding. These debts can be imputed to you personally.

Qualifying as a Foreign Corporation

A corporation conducting business in a state other than its state of incorporation is deemed a foreign corporation in the state in which it is a guest. States generally require foreign corporations conducting business within their borders to qualify as foreign corporations. This process of registering in a foreign state is known as qualification. What constitutes "conducting business" for the purposes of determining the qualification threshold will differ from state to state.

Qualifying as a foreign corporation closely mirrors the process of incorporation: Corporations must typically file their articles of incorporation in the foreign state, along with an additional filing that includes information specific to the foreign state, such as the resident agent in the foreign state. The filing fees for qualification are always at least the same as for filing articles of incorporation, but often are more.

The decision whether to qualify in a foreign state must be made cautiously. Once qualified, a corporation must file periodic corporate reports in the foreign state, will likely need to file tax returns and pay taxes in the foreign state, and must have a local agent appointed in the foreign state. Also, qualification in a foreign state makes it much easier for creditors to serve process and bring lawsuits against your corporation in the foreign state.

Maintaining Corporate Formalities

Corporations must honor certain ongoing formalities in their internal governance and administration. Such formalities are required by state law and by the corporation's bylaws. Examples of ongoing corporate formalities include:

- Annual and special meeting must be properly noticed (or participants must execute waivers of notice).
- Corporations must hold annual meetings of shareholders and annual meetings of directors, unless the corporation is a close corporation.
- Managers must prepare written minutes of all corporate meetings.
- Shareholder and director votes must meet quorum requirements.
- Removal of directors and officers must be effected by a proper vote.
- Directors and shareholders must respect the boundaries of conflicts of interest when entering personal transactions with the corporation.

Annual Meetings of Shareholders

The shareholders' single greatest responsibility is the election of corporate directors. The shareholders elect directors at each annual meeting of shareholders. The date for the annual meeting of shareholders is usually set forth in the bylaws. Some corporations prefer to have their shareholders' meeting a few months after the end of their fiscal year. Thus, shareholders and managers may discuss the company's financial performance for the previous year.

Because the date for annual shareholder meetings is designated in the bylaws, no formal notice of such meetings is typically required. However, prudence dictates that a reminder be distributed to shareholders advising them of the meeting. Annual meetings of directors can be held at the same time and place, and should follow immediately after the shareholders' meeting.

A quorum of shareholders must be present in order to hold a valid shareholder vote. Quorum requirements prevent a small minority of shareholders from taking control of a corporation. Keep in mind that corporations may have multiple classes of shares—and some classes do not necessarily have voting rights.

State law typically dictates that a majority of the outstanding voting shares constitutes a quorum, but corporate organizers can reduce the number of shares that constitute a quorum by adding an appropriate provision in the bylaws. A provision reducing the quorum to 40 percent of outstanding shares would read, "The presence in person or by proxy of the holders of Forty Percent of the shares entitled to vote at any meeting of Shareholders shall constitute a quorum for the transaction of business." Bear in mind that the minimum allowable quorum will differ from state to state. For smaller corporations, the quorum should be set to a simple majority.

Special Meetings of Shareholders

Special meetings of shareholders may be called at any time. Special shareholder meetings, more often than not, are called in order to make changes to the board of directors—either by removing the entire board, removing one or more directors, or filling a vacancy in the board. In order to call a special meeting the following requirements must be met:

- The shareholder or shareholders calling the special meeting must collectively own a minimum percentage of a corporation's outstanding shares. The minimum differs from state to state; it is typically around five or ten percent.

- Directors and officers may also call special shareholders' meetings.

- The party calling the meeting typically issues a written document called a "call" to the corporate secretary, who then is charged with the responsibility of noticing the meeting. See Appendix A for a sample call letter.

- Notice must be delivered to all shareholders advising them of the time and place of the meeting and of the proposals to be presented. See Appendix A for a sample Notice of Special Shareholder Meeting.

Appearance at Shareholder Meetings by Proxy

A proxy is an authorization by one shareholder giving another person the right to vote the shareholder's shares. Proxy also refers to the document granting such authority. Proxy rules are typically outlined in state law and a corporation's bylaws.

Proxies can state the period of time for which they are effective. If no duration is stated, the proxy will lapse automatically by state law. A proxy that states no duration remains effective for eleven months in California[7] and three years in Delaware.[8]

A proxy may either give the proxy holder absolute authority to vote the shares as they wish, or a long-form proxy may state the specific proposals for which the proxy is given. In some states, larger corporations require long-form proxies. The size of the corporation that triggers the heightened requirements differs from state to state.

See forms 11 and 12 in Appendix A for illustrative sample proxy forms.

Recording Meetings by Preparing Minutes

Annual and special meetings of shareholders and of directors must be recorded. The written record of the actions taken at a such meetings are called minutes. Minutes are very simple to prepare, and are often quite short. There are several sample minutes in Appendix A that cover a wide range of corporate actions. Minutes of meetings should always contain the following information:

- The nature of the meeting, i.e., shareholder's or director's meeting, annual or special meeting;
- That the meeting was either called by notice or that the persons voting waived such notice by executing a written waiver of notice;
- Who was present at the meeting;
- The date, time, and place of the meeting;
- Who served as chairperson of the meeting;

---

7. Cal. Corp. Code § 705(b).
8. Del. Gen. Corp. Law § 212.

- What actions were taken at the meeting, i.e., election of directors, issuance of stock and purchase of real estate; and
- When in doubt, simply record the foregoing information at the meeting in plain, conversational English.

Holding Votes by Written Consent

Subject to certain restrictions, shareholders or directors may take an action without a meeting if their action is memorialized in a written consent. A written consent is simply a formal written document that sets forth a corporate action to be taken, and it is signed by the shareholders or directors consenting to the action. Some directors and managers find written consents to be invaluable—they are quicker, easier, cheaper, and more convenient than a fully noticed shareholders' or directors' meeting. Actions taken by written consent do not require minutes because the written consent itself serves as a memorandum of the action. See Form 16 in Appendix A for an illustrative sample form.

Written consents must be unanimous in some states for some corporate actions, such as the election of directors, or the election to become a close corporation, or amendment of the articles of incorporation.

A written consent should include the following information:

- The nature of the action taken, i.e., whether the action is a shareholders' or directors' action;
- A statement that the shareholders or directors taking the action waive notice of a meeting;
- What actions were taken, i.e., election of directors, amendment of bylaws, election to be a close corporation, approval of stock option plan, purchase of real estate, etc.; and
- When in doubt, simply record the foregoing information at the meeting in plain, conversational English.

Annual Meetings of Directors

Directors of a corporation should meet annually, whether or not required by law. The date for the annual meeting of directors is ordinarily set forth in the corporate bylaws. Typically, the directors' annual meeting follows immediately after the shareholders' annual meeting. At this meeting, the directors select officers to serve until the next annual meeting and can take any other necessary corporate action.

Because the date for annual directors' meetings is designated in the bylaws, no formal notice of such meetings is typically required. However, prudence dictates that a reminder be distributed to directors advising of the meeting.

A quorum of directors must be present in order to effect a director vote. Quorum requirements prevent a small minority of directors from taking control of a corporation.

State law typically dictates that a majority of the directors currently serving constitutes a quorum, but corporate organizers can require a supermajority of directors be required to effect votes on particular corporate actions. A supermajority is a percentage higher than a 50 percent "simple" majority. For example, organizers can require that a unanimous director vote be required to dissolve the corporation, or to approve a merger of the corporation with another entity.

Special Meetings of Directors

Like special meetings of shareholders, special meetings of directors may be called at any time. Because directors have ultimate authority over the management of a corporation, special meetings of directors may be called for any purpose. See Form 18 in Appendix A for a sample Notice of Special Meeting of Board of Directors. The procedure for calling a special meeting of directors is as follows:

- Directors or officers have the authority to call special meeting of directors.

- The party calling the meeting typically issues a written notice called a "call" to the corporate secretary, who then is charged with the responsibility of noticing the meeting. See Form 17 in Appendix A for a sample call letter.

- Notice must be delivered to all directors advising them of the time and place of the meeting and of the proposals to be presented.

Annual Reporting Requirements

All states require corporations to file periodic reports with the secretary of state's office, or its equivalent department. A corporation files such reports in its state of incorporation and in states in which it is qualified as a foreign corporation. Some states, including California and Alaska, have recently relaxed their reporting requirements; these states have moved to biennial filing of corporate reports (every two years). Annual report filing fees, due dates, late penalties, and information requirements differ from state to state.

Some states, such as California, Georgia, and Arkansas, now offer online filing of periodic reports. Check the website of the appropriate state office, listed in the State Reference Tables in Appendix B, to see if your state of incorporation offers an online filing program. You may reasonably expect that online filing will be offered by more states in the near future.

For a more in-depth, detailed explanation of observing and maintaining corporate formalities and paperwork, consider *The Essential Corporation Handbook* by Carl R.J. Sniffen. The book features checklists to keep your formalities up-to-date and more strategies on how to avoid personal liability. Visit:

Oasis Press
http://www.oasispress.com

Amending Articles of Incorporation & Bylaws

Shareholders may amend a corporation's articles of incorporation. The shareholders vote on proposed amendments either at an annual meeting of shareholders or at a special meeting called for that purpose. Alternatively, the shareholders may approve an amendment by written consent. An amendment to a corporation's articles of incorporation must be filed with the secretary of state. The amendment is not legally effective until the secretary of state accepts the filing. Some states require either a supermajority vote or a unanimous vote to approve particular amendments. The state's great area of concern is amendments that alter or dilute the rights of existing shareholders, such as amendments authorizing additional shares (which dilute existing shareholders).

Common amendments to articles of incorporation include the following:

- A provision changing the name of the corporation;
- A provision increasing the number of authorized shares of the corporation;
- A provision electing to make the corporation a close corporation; and
- A provision adopting an additional class of shares.

Typically, both directors and shareholders enjoy the right to amend a corporation's bylaws. Some states place partial restrictions on the right of directors to amend bylaws, but each state will differ. A corporation's bylaws contain provisions outlining a procedure for amending bylaws. Because bylaws are not filed with the state, amendments to bylaws are not filed with the state. Amendments to bylaws become effective immediately upon their adoption by either the board of directors or by shareholders.

Common amendments to bylaws include the following:

- A provision increasing or decreasing the number of directors; and
- A provision changing the date for the corporation's annual meetings.

Dissolution: Ending Your Corporation's Life

A corporation has a perpetual life unless that life is cut short by dissolution. A dissolution is the process of shutting down a corporation, settling its affairs, paying its creditors, distributing its remaining assets to its shareholders, and ending its life. A dissolution may be one of three types.

- A voluntary dissolution is the intentional dissolution of a corporation by its own management.
- An administrative dissolution is a dissolution ordered either by the secretary of state, other equivalent department, or other authorized state official.
- A judicial dissolution is one ordered by a court of law.

Voluntary Dissolution

A corporation's directors may vote for voluntary dissolution either at a meeting of directors or by written consent. A notice of dissolution or application for dissolution form is then filed with the secretary of state. In some states, the secretary of state will not approve the voluntary dissolution of either a corporation that is not in good standing, or a corporation with an outstanding tax liability. This is an interesting paradox because the eventual penalty for delinquency in corporate filings is administrative dissolution.

Administrative Dissolution

The secretary of state enjoys the power to order a corporation's administrative dissolution. The secretary of state may exercise this power if a corporation becomes seriously delinquent in meeting its statutory requirements, such as periodic filing and tax reporting requirements. What constitutes a delinquency serious enough to warrant an administrative dissolution differs from state to state. Some states allow a reinstatement of good standing following an administrative dissolution, upon a proper filing.

Judicial Dissolution

A court of law may order the judicial dissolution of a corporation upon the request of a state attorney general, shareholder, or creditor. A shareholder, for example, may bring an action to dissolve a corporation if the corporation is committing a waste of corporate assets, or if the shareholder's rights are being abused by other shareholders, or in the case of a voting deadlock among shareholders or directors.

Always endeavor to avoid dissolution because it can lead to a failure of a corporation's liability protection. Always exercise great care when voluntarily dissolving a corporation. Never allow a corporation with debt to become dissolved. If you are a shareholder of a dissolved corporation with outstanding liabilities, those liabilities may be attributed to you.

Sample Forms

This appendix features more than 20 sample forms of various corporate paperwork. In it, you will see samples of articles of incorporation, letters, bylaws, and notices. All of these sample forms are available so you can modify them to suit your needs and to use them as models. For your convenience, you can also find these model documents at this website.

LearnAboutLaw.com

http://www.learnaboutlaw.com

The last two forms are blank corporate tax forms from the IRS. You are welcome to copy them from this book, or you can visit the IRS' website for these forms, as well as other necessary forms for your corporation.

Internal Revenue Service

http://www.irs.gov/plain/forms_pubs/index.html

Remember these samples are not to take the place of your attorney's legal advice; they are simply intended to help you become more knowledgeable and familiar with corporate formalities and recordkeeping.

Form 1: Form LLC-1 – Limited Liability Company Articles of Organization (for California) Sample

State of California
Bill Jones
Secretary of State

File#_____

LIMITED LIABILITY COMPANY
ARTICLES OF ORGANIZATION

A $70.00 filing fee must accompany this form.
IMPORTANT – Read instructions before completing this form.

This Space For Filing Use Only

1. Name of the limited liability company (end the name with the words "Limited Liability Company," " Ltd. Liability Co.," or the abbreviations "LLC" or "L.L.C.")

2. The purpose of the limited liability company is to engage in any lawful act or activity for which a limited liability company may be organized under the Beverly-Killea limited liability company act.

3. Name the agent for service of process and check the appropriate provision below:

    _____ which is

    [ ] an individual residing in California. Proceed to item 4.

    [ ] a corporation which has filed a certificate pursuant to section 1505. Proceed to item 5.

4. If an individual, California address of the agent for service of process:
    Address:

    City: State: **CA**   Zip Code:

5. The limited liability company will be managed by: **(check one)**

    [ ] one manager   **[ ] more than one manager**   **[ ] limited liability company members**

6. Other matters to be included in this certificate may be set forth on separate attached pages and are made a part of this certificate. Other matters may include the latest date on which the limited liability company is to dissolve.

7. Number of pages attached, if any:

    Type of business of the limited liability company.

    DECLARATION: It is hereby declared that I am the person who executed this instrument, which execution is my act and deed.

    _____   _____
    Signature of Organizer   Type or Print Name of Organizer

    _____
    Date

SEC/STATE (REV. 1/99)   FORM LLC-1 – FILING FEE $70.00
                                               Approved by Secretary of State

INSTRUCTIONS FOR COMPLETING THE ARTICLES OF ORGANIZATION (LLC-1)

DO NOT ALTER THIS FORM

Type or legibly print in black ink.

Professional limited liability companies are prohibited from forming or registering in California.

- Attach the fee for filing the Articles of Organization (LLC-1) with the Secretary of State. The fee is seventy dollars ($70).

- Make check(s) payable to the Secretary of State.

- Send the executed document and filing fee to:

  California Secretary of State
  Limited Liability Company Unit
  P.O. Box 944228
  Sacramento, CA 94244-2280

- Fill in the items as follows:

Item 1. Enter the name of the limited liability company. The name shall contain the words "Limited Liability Company," or the abbreviations "LLC" or "L.L.C." The words "Limited" and "Company" may be abbreviated to "Ltd." and "Co." The name of the limited liability company may not contain the words "bank," "trust," "trustee," incorporated," "inc.," "corporation," or "corp.," and shall not contain the words "insurer" or "insurance company" or any other words suggesting that it is in the business of issuing policies of insurance and assuming insurance risks. (Section 17052)

Item 2. Execution of this document confirms the following statement which has been preprinted on the form and may not be altered: "The purpose of the limited liability company is to engage in any lawful act or activity for which a limited liability company may be organized under the Beverly-Killea Limited Liability Company Act." Provisions limiting or restricting the business of the limited liability company may be included as an attachment.

Item 3. Enter the name of the agent for service of process. The agent for service of process must be an individual residing in California or a corporation which has filed a certificate pursuant to California Corporations Code Section 1505. Check the appropriate provision.

Item 4. If an individual is designated as the agent for service of process, enter an address in California. Do not enter "in care of" (c/o) or abbreviate the name of the city. DO NOT enter an address if a corporation is designated as the agent for service of process.

Item 5. Check the appropriate provision indicating whether the limited liability company is to be managed by one manager, more than one manager, or the limited liability company members. Section 17051(a)(5).

Item 6. The Articles of Organization (LLC-1) may include other matters that the person filing the Articles of Organization determines to include. Other matters may include the latest date on which the limited liability company is to dissolve. If other matters are to be included check the box in this item and attach one or more pages setting forth the other matters.

Item 7. Indicate the total number of additional pages attached. All attachments should be 8½" x 11", one-sided and legible.

For informational purposes only, briefly describe the type of business that constitutes the principal business activity of the limited liability company. Note restrictions in the rendering of professional services by Limited Liability Companies. Professional services are defined in California Corporations Code, Section 13401(a) as: "Any type of professional services that may be lawfully rendered only pursuant to a license, certification, or registration authorized by the Business and Professions Code or the Chiropractic Act."

Declaration: The Articles of Organization (LLC-1) shall be executed with an original signature of the organizer. A facsimile or photocopy of the signature is not acceptable for the purpose of filing with the Secretary of State.

The person executing the Articles of Organization (LLC-1) need not be a member or manager of the limited liability company.

If an entity is signing the Articles of Organization (LLC-1), the person who signs for the entity must note the exact entity name, his/her name, and his/her position.

If an attorney-in-fact is signing the Articles of Organization (LLC-1), the signature must be followed by the words "Attorney-in-fact for (name of person)."

If a trust is signing the Articles of Organization (LLC-1), the articles must be signed by a trustee as follows: _____, trustee for_____trust (including the date of the trust, if applicable). Example: Mary Todd, trustee of the Lincoln Family Trust (U/T/A 5-1-94).

- Statutory provisions can be found in Section 17051 of the California Corporations Code, unless otherwise indicated.

- For further information contact the Limited Liability Company Unit at (916) 653-3795.

Form 2: Delaware Articles of Incorporation Sample

Certificate of Incorporation of [Corporation Name]

FIRST: The name of the corporation is [Corporation Name].

SECOND: Its registered office in the State of Delaware is located at [Delaware corporations must have a registered agent in DE, place registered office address here]. The registered agent in charge thereof is [insert name of registered agent].

THIRD: The purpose of the corporation is to engage in any lawful activity for which corporations may be organized under the General Corporation Law of Delaware.

FOURTH: The total number of shares of stock that the corporation is authorized to issue is 3,000 shares having a par value of $0.0001 per share. [Note: DE corporations with more than 3,000 authorized shares pay their annual franchise tax fees according to a complex formula. Such fees are not terribly expensive, but see the DE Department of Corporations' website for information before authorizing more than 3,000 shares].

FIFTH: The business and affairs of the corporation shall be managed by or under the direction of the board of directors, and the directors need not be elected by ballot unless required by the bylaws of the corporation.

SIXTH: The Corporation shall be perpetual unless otherwise decided by a majority of the board of directors.

SEVENTH: In furtherance and not in limitation of the powers conferred by the laws of Delaware, the board of directors is authorized to amend or repeal the bylaws.

EIGHTH: The Corporation reserves the right to amend or repeal any provision in this Certificate of Incorporation in the manner prescribed by the Laws of Delaware.

NINTH: The incorporator is [insert name of Incorporator]. The powers of the incorporator are to file this certificate of incorporation, approve the by-laws of the corporation and elect the initial directors.

TENTH: To the fullest extent permitted by the Delaware General Corporation Law a director of this corporation shall not be liable to the corporation or its stockholders for monetary damages for breach of fiduciary duty as a director.

I, [insert name of Incorporator], for the purpose of forming a corporation under the laws of the State of Delaware do make and file this certificate, and do certify that the facts herein stated are true; and have accordingly signed below, on [Date].

Signed and Attested to by:

_____

[Incorporator Name]

Incorporator

Form 3: California Articles of Incorporation Sample

Articles of Incorporation of [Corporation Name]

1. The name of this corporation is [insert corporation name].

2. The purpose of the corporation is to engage in any lawful act or activity for which a corporation may be organized under the General Corporation Law of California other than the banking business, the trust company business or the practice of a profession permitted to be incorporated by the California Corporations Code.

3. The name and address in the State of California of this Corporation's initial agent for service of process is [insert name and address of initial agent for service of process].

4. This corporation is authorized to issue only one class of shares of stock; and the total number of shares which this corporation is authorized to issue is one million (1,000,000) shares.

5. The liability of the directors of the corporation for monetary damages shall be eliminated to the fullest extent permissible under California law.

Dated: _____

_____

[Incorporator Name]

Incorporator

Form 4: Optional Provisions for Inclusion in Articles of Incorporation Sample

a. Clause establishing a class of voting common stock and a class of non-voting common stock:

This corporation is authorized to issue two classes of shares: "Class A Common Stock" and "Class B Common Stock." This corporation may issue 1,000,000 shares of Class A Common Stock, and 500,000 shares of Class B Common Stock. The Class B Common Stock has no voting rights. The Class A Common Stock has exclusive voting rights except as otherwise provided by law.

b. Clause establishing a class of voting common stock and a class of preferred stock:

This corporation is authorized to issue two classes of shares: "Common Stock" and "Preferred Stock." This corporation may issue 1,000,000 shares of Common Stock, and 500,000 shares of Preferred Stock. The Common Stock has voting rights. The Preferred Stock has no voting rights except as otherwise provided by law.

The Preferred Stock has a liquidation preference. Upon the liquidation or dissolution of the corporation, holders of the Preferred Stock are entitled to receive out of the assets available for distribution to shareholders, before any payment to the holders of the Common Stock, the sum of $___ per share. If the assets of the corporation are insufficient to pay this liquidation preference to the Preferred Stock, all of the entire remaining assets shall be paid to holders of the Preferred Stock, and holders of the Common Stock shall receive nothing. After the liquidation preference has been paid or set apart for holders of the Preferred Stock, the remaining assets shall be paid to holders of the Common Stock.

The Preferred Stock has a dividend preference. Holders of the Preferred Stock are entitled to receive dividends on a noncumulative basis at the rate of $___ per share, as and when declared by the board of from funds legally available for dividends and distributions. The holders of the Common Stock may not receive dividends or other distributions during any fiscal year of the corporation until dividends on the Preferred Stock in the total amount of $___ per share during that fiscal year have been declared and paid, or set apart for payment. The payment of such dividends is discretionary, and the holders of the Preferred Stock shall not enjoy a right to dividends if such dividends are not declared, even if the corporation has sufficient funds to lawfully pay such dividends.

Form 5: Letter to Secretary of State Accompanying Articles of Incorporation Sample

Michael D. Spadaccini
123 Elm Street
San Francisco, California 94107
(415) 555-1212

September 28, 2001

State of Delaware
Division of Corporations
401 Federal Street, Suite 4
Dover, Delaware 19901

To Whom It May Concern,

Enclosed you will find articles of incorporation for Banquo Acquisition Corporation, a corporation that I wish to file in Delaware.

I have enclosed a filing fee of $74.00. Please return any necessary papers in the envelope that I have provided.

Yours truly,

_____

Michael Spadaccini

[Note: This letter is a version appropriate for use in Delaware, but can be modified for use in any state.]

Form 6: Letter to Registered Agent Sample

Michael D. Spadaccini
123 Elm Street
San Francisco, California 94107
(415) 555-1212

September 28, 2001

Harvard Business Services, Inc.
25 Greystone Manor
Lewes, DE 19958

To Whom It May Concern,

I have enclosed a copy of articles of incorporation I am filing today. As you can see, I have used you as our registered agents in the state of Delaware.

Please use the following contact information:

Banquo Acquisition Corporation
c/o Michael Spadaccini
801 Minnesota Street, Suite 7
San Francisco, CA 94107
Phone (415) 282-7901

I have enclosed a check for $50.00 to cover the first year's services.

Yours truly,

_____

Michael Spadaccini

Form 7: Action By Incorporator Appointing Directors and Approving Bylaws
Sample

Minutes of Action of Incorporator Taken Without a Meeting By Written Consent

The following action is taken by the incorporator of Olde Craft, Inc., by written consent, without a meeting on the date specified below.

The following resolution approving a form of bylaws for the governance of this corporation is adopted:

RESOLVED, that the bylaws presented to the incorporator be adopted as the bylaws of this corporation, and that a copy of those bylaws shall be inserted in the minute book of this corporation.

The following resolution electing the directors of the corporation is adopted:

RESOLVED, that pursuant to the foregoing bylaws, authorizing THREE directors, the following persons are hereby appointed as directors of this corporation for the ensuing year and until their successor[s] have been elected and qualified.

John Jones

John Smith

John Miller

The undersigned, the incorporator of this corporation, consents to the foregoing action.

Dated: _____

_____

Michael Spadaccini, Incorporator

Form 8: Corporate Bylaws Sample

Bylaws of [Corporation Name]

Part A. Board of Directors

1. Subject to state law and the articles of incorporation, the business and affairs of this corporation shall be managed by and all corporate powers shall be exercised by or under the direction of the board of directors.

2. Each director shall exercise such powers and otherwise perform such duties in good faith, and in the manner provided for by law.

3. This corporation shall have [insert the number of directors] directors. This number may be changed by amendment of the bylaws, adopted by the vote or written consent of a majority of shareholders entitled to vote. The term "board of directors" as used in these bylaws means the number of directors authorized in this paragraph, even if that number is one.

4. Directors shall be elected at each annual meeting of the shareholders to hold office until the next annual meeting, subject to any rights of shareholders outlined in any shareholder's agreement. Each director, including a director elected to fill a vacancy, shall hold office until expiration of the term for which elected and until a successor has been elected and qualified.

5. Vacancies in the board of directors may be filled by a majority of the remaining directors, though less than a quorum, or by a sole remaining director. Each director so elected shall hold office until the next annual meeting of the shareholders and until a successor has been elected and qualified.

6. A vacancy in the board of directors shall be deemed to exist in the event of the death, resignation, or removal of any director, or if the shareholders fail, at any meeting of the shareholders at which any directors are elected, to elect the full number of authorized directors. The shareholders may elect a director or directors to fill any vacancy or vacancies not filled by the directors, but any such election by written consent shall require a consent of a majority of the outstanding shares entitled to vote. Any director may resign effective upon giving written notice to the President, or the Secretary, unless the notice specifies a later time for that resignation to become effective. If the resignation of a director is effective at a future time, the shareholders may elect a successor to take office when the resignation becomes effective. No reduction of the authorized number of directors shall have the effect of removing any director before the director's term of office expires.

7. The entire board of directors or any individual director named may be removed from office as provided by state law. In such a case, the shareholder(s) may elect a successor director to fill such vacancy for the remaining unexpired term of the director so removed.

8. Regular meetings of the board of directors shall be held at any place within or without the state that has been designated from time to time by resolution of the board. In the absence of such resolution, regular meetings shall be held at the principal executive office of the corporation. Special meetings of the board shall be held at any place within or without the state that has been designated in the notice of the meeting, or, if not stated in the notice or there is no notice, at the principal executive office of the corporation. Any meeting, regular or special, may be held by conference telephone or similar communication equipment, so long as all directors participating in such meeting can hear one another, and all such directors shall be deemed to have been present in person at such meeting.

9. Immediately following each annual meeting of shareholders, the board of directors shall hold a regular meeting for the purpose of organization, the election of officers and the transaction of other business. Notice of this meeting shall not be required. Minutes of any meeting of the board, or any committee of the board, shall be maintained by the Secretary or other officer designated for that purpose.

10. Other regular meetings of the board of directors shall be held without call at such time as shall from time to time be fixed by the board of directors. Such regular meetings may be held without notice, provided the time and place of such meetings has been fixed by the board of directors, and further provided the notice of any change in the time of such meeting shall be given to all the directors. Notice of a change in the determination of the time shall be given to each director in the same manner as notice for special meetings of the board of directors. If said day falls upon a holiday, such meetings shall be held on the next succeeding day thereafter.

11. Special meetings of the board of directors for any purpose or purposes may be called at any time by the Chairman of the Board or the President or any Vice President or the Secretary or any two directors.

12. Notice of the time and place for special meetings shall be delivered personally or by telephone to each director or sent by first class mail or telegram, charges prepaid, addressed to each director at his or her address as it is shown in the records of the corporation. In case such notice is mailed, it shall be deposited in the United States mail at least ten (10) days prior to the time of holding of the meeting. In case such notice is delivered personally, or by telephone or telegram, it shall be delivered personally or by telephone or to the telegram company at least forty-eight (48) hours prior to the time of the holding of the meeting. Any oral notice given personally or by telephone may be communicated to either the director or to a person at the office of the director who the person giving the notice has reason to believe will promptly be communicated to the director. The notice need not specify the purpose of the meeting, nor the place, if the meeting is to be held at the principal executive of the corporation.

13. The transactions of any meeting of the Board of directors, however called, noticed, or wherever held, shall be as valid as though had at a meeting duly held after the regular call and notice if a quorum be present and if, either before or after the meeting, each of

Form 8: Corporate Bylaws Sample (continued)

the directors not present signs a written waiver of notice, a consent to holding the meeting or an approval of the minutes thereof. Waiver of notices or consents need not specify the purpose of the meeting. All such waivers, consents and approvals shall be filed with the corporate records or made part of the minutes of the meeting. Notice of a meeting shall also be deemed given to any director who attends the meeting without protesting, prior thereto or at its commencement, the lack of notice to such director. A majority of the authorized number of directors shall constitute a quorum for the transaction of business, except to adjourn as otherwise provided in these bylaws. Every act or decision done or made by a majority of the directors present at a meeting duly held at which a quorum was present shall be regarded as the act of the board of directors.

14. A majority of the directors present, whether or not constituting a quorum, may adjourn any meeting to another time and place.

15. Notice of the time and place of the holding of an adjourned meeting need not be given, unless the meeting is adjourned for more than twenty-four (24) hours, in which case notice of such time and place shall be given prior to the time of the adjourned meeting to the directors who were not present at the time of the adjournment.

16. Any action required or permitted to be taken by the board of directors may be taken given a meeting with the same force and effect as if taken by unanimous vote of directors, if authorized by a writing signed individually or collectively by all members of the board. Such consent shall be filed with the regular minutes of the board.

17. Directors and members of a directors' committee may receive such compensation and such reimbursement of expenses, as may be fixed or determined by resolution of the board of directors. Nothing herein contained shall be construed to preclude any director from serving the corporation in any other capacity as an officer, employee, or otherwise, and receiving compensation for such services.

18. Committees of the board may be appointed by resolution passed by a majority of the whole board. Committees shall be composed of two (2) or more members of the board and shall have such powers of the board as may be expressly delegated to them by resolution of the board of directors. The board may designate one (1) or more directors as alternate members of any committee, who may replace any absent member at any meeting of the committee. Committees shall have such powers of the board of directors as may be expressly delegated to it by resolution of the board of directors.

19. The board of directors from time to time may elect one (1) or more persons to be advisory directors, who shall not by such appointment be members of the board of directors. Advisory directors shall be available from time to time to perform special assignments specified by the President, to attend meetings of the board of directors upon invitation and to furnish consultation to the board. The period during which the title shall be held may be prescribed by the board of directors. If no period is prescribed, title shall be held at the pleasure of the board.

Part B. Officers

20. The principal officers of the corporation shall be a President, a Secretary, and a Chief Financial Officer who may also be called Treasurer. The corporation may also have, at the discretion of the board of directors, one or more Vice Presidents, one or more Assistant Secretaries, and such other officers as may be appointed in accordance with paragraph 22 of these bylaws. One person may hold two or more offices.

21. The principal officers of the corporation, except such officers as may be appointed in accordance with paragraph 22 of these bylaws, shall be chosen by the board of directors, and each shall serve at the pleasure of the board of directors, subject to the rights, if any, of an officer under any contract of employment.

22. The board of directors may empower the President to appoint and remove such officers (other than the principal officers) as the business of the corporation may require, each of whom shall hold office for such period, have such authority and perform such duties as are provided in the bylaws or as the board of directors may from time to time determine.

23. Subject to the rights, if any, of an officer under any contract of employment, any officer may be removed, either with or without cause, by a majority of the directors at that time in office, at any regular or special meeting of the board, or, excepting the case of an officer chosen by the board of directors, by any officer upon whom such power of removal may be conferred by the board of directors.

24. A vacancy in any office because of death, resignation, removal, disqualification, or any other cause shall be filled in the manner prescribed in these bylaws for regular appointments to such office.

25. The Chairman of the board, if an officer be elected, shall, if present, preside at all meetings of the board of directors and exercise and perform such other powers and duties as may from time to time be assigned to him by the board of directors or prescribed by the bylaws. If there is no President, the Chairman of the board shall in addition be the Chief Executive Officer of the corporation and shall have the powers and duties prescribed in paragraph 26 of these bylaws.

26. Subject to such supervisory powers, if any, as may be given by the board of directors to the Chairman of the board, if there be such an officer, the President shall be the Chief Executive Officer of the corporation and shall, subject to the control of the board of directors, have general supervision, direction and control of the business and the officers of the corporation. He or she shall preside at all the meetings of the shareholders and, in the absence of the Chairman of the board, of if there be none, at all meetings of shareholders and, in the absence of the Chairman of the board, or if there be none, at all meetings of the board of directors. He or she shall have the general powers and duties of management usually vested in the office of President of a corporation, shall be ex officio a member of all the standing committees, including the executive committee, if any, and shall have such other powers and duties as may be described by the board of directors or the bylaws.

Form 8: Corporate Bylaws Sample (continued)

27. In the absence or disability of the President, the Vice Presidents, if any, in order of their rank as fixed by the board of directors, shall perform all the duties of the President, and so acting shall have all the powers of, and be subject to the restriction upon, the President. The Vice Presidents shall have such other powers and perform such other duties as from time to time may be prescribed for them respectively by the board of directors or the bylaws, the President, or the Chairman of the board.

28. The Secretary shall keep or cause to be kept at the principal executive office or such other place as the board of directors may order, a book of minutes of all meetings of directors, committees of directors, and shareholders, with the time and place of holding, whether regular or special, and, if special, how authorized, the notice thereof given, the names of those present at directors and committee meetings, the number of shares present or represented at shareholders meetings, and the proceedings thereof. The Secretary shall keep or cause to be kept at the principal office or at the office of the corporation's transfer agent, a share register, or duplicate share register, showing the names of the shareholders and their addresses; the number of classes of shares held by each; the number and date of certificates issued for the same; and the number and date of cancellation of every certificate surrendered for cancellation. The Secretary shall give or cause to be given notice of all meetings of the shareholders and of the board of directors required by the bylaws or by law to be given, shall keep the seal of the corporation in safe custody, and shall have such other powers and perform such other duties as may be prescribed by the board of directors or by the bylaws.

29. The Chief Financial Officer shall keep and maintain, or cause to be kept and maintained, adequate and correct books and records of accounts of the properties and business transactions of the corporation, including accounts of its assets, liabilities, receipts, disbursements, gains, losses, capital, retained earnings and shares. The books of account shall at all reasonable times be open to inspection by any director. The Chief Financial Officer shall deposit all moneys and other valuables in the name and to the credit of the corporation with such depositories as may be designated by the board of directors. He or she shall disburse the funds of the corporation as may be ordered by the board of directors, shall render to the President and directors, whenever they request it, an account of all of his transactions as Chief Financial Officer and of the financial condition of the corporation, and shall have other powers and perform such other duties as may be prescribed by the board of directors or the bylaws.

Part C. Shareholders

30. Meetings of shareholders shall be held at any place designated by the board of directors. In the absence of any such designation, shareholders' meetings shall be held at the principal executive office of the corporation.

31. The annual meeting of the shareholders shall be held on March 1. If this day be a legal holiday, then the meeting shall be held on the next succeeding business day, at the same

time. At the annual meeting, the shareholders shall elect a board of directors, report the affairs of the corporation, and transact such other business as may properly be brought before the meeting. If the above date is inconvenient, the annual meeting of shareholders shall be held each year on a date and at a time designated by the board of directors within twenty (20) days of the above date upon proper notice to all shareholders.

32. A special meeting of the shareholders, for any purpose or purposes whatsoever, may be called at any time by the board of directors, or by the Chairman of the board of directors, or by the President, or by one or more shareholders holding shares in the aggregate entitled to cast not less than 10% of the votes at any such meeting. If a special meeting is called by any person or persons other than the board of directors, the request shall be in writing, specifying the time of such meeting and the general nature of the business proposed to be transacted, and shall be delivered personally or sent by registered mail or by telegraphic or other facsimile transmission to the Chairman of the board, the President, any Vice President or the Secretary of the corporation. The officer receiving such request shall forthwith cause notice to be given to the shareholders entitled to vote, in accordance with the provisions of paragraphs 33 and 34 of these bylaws, that a meeting will be held at the time requested by the person or persons calling the meeting, not less than thirty-five (35) nor more than sixty (60) days after the receipt of the request. If the notice is not given within twenty (20) days after receipt of the request, the person or persons requesting the meeting may give the notice in the manner provided in these bylaws. Nothing contained in this paragraph shall be construed as limiting, fixing or affecting the time when a meeting of shareholders called by action of the board of directors may be held.

33. Notice of meetings, annual or special, shall be given in writing not less than ten (10) nor more than sixty (60) days before the date of the meeting, to shareholders entitled to vote thereat by the Secretary or the Assistant Secretary, or if there be no such officer, or in the case of his or her neglect or refusal, by any director or shareholder. Such notices or any reports shall be given personally or by mail, or other means of communication as provided by state law, and shall be sent to the shareholder's address appearing on the books of the corporation, or supplied by him or her to the corporation for the purposes of notice. Notice of any meeting of shareholders shall specify the place, date and hour of the meeting and (i) in the case of a special meeting, the general nature of the business to be transacted, and no other business may be transacted, or (ii) in the case of an annual meeting, those matters which the board of directors, at the date of the mailing of notice, intends to present for action by the shareholders. At any meetings where directors are elected, notice shall include the names of the nominees, if any, intended at the date of notice to be presented by the management for election.

34. The presence in person or by proxy of the holders of a majority of the shares entitled to vote at any meeting of shareholders shall constitute a quorum for the transaction of business. The shareholders present at a duly called or held meeting at which a quorum is present may continue to do business until adjournment, notwithstanding the withdrawal of

Form 8: Corporate Bylaws Sample (continued)

enough shareholders to leave less than a quorum, if any action taken (other than adjournment) is approved by at least a majority of the shares required to constitute a quorum.

35. Any shareholders' meeting, annual or special, whether or not a quorum is present, may be adjourned from time to time by the vote of the majority of the shares represented at such meeting, either in person or by proxy, but in the absence of a quorum, no other business may be transacted at such meeting. When any meeting of shareholders, wither annual or special, is adjourned to another time or place, notice need not be given of the adjourned meeting if the time and place thereof are announced at a meeting at which the adjournment is taken, unless a new record date for the adjourned meeting is fixed, or unless a new record date for the adjourned meeting is fixed, or unless the adjournment is for more than forty-five (45) days from the date set for the original meeting, in which case the board of directors shall set a new record date. Notice of any such adjourned meeting shall be given to each shareholder of record entitled to vote at the adjourned meeting in accordance with the provisions of paragraph 33 of these bylaws.

36. The transactions at any meeting of shareholders, wither annual or special, however called and noticed, and wherever held, shall be as valid as though had at a meeting duly held after regular call and notice, if a quorum be present either in person or by proxy, and if, either before of after the meeting, each person entitled to vote, not present in person or by proxy, signs a written waiver of notice or a consent to a holding of the meeting, or any approval of the minutes thereof. All such waivers, consents or approvals shall be filed with the corporate records or made a part of the minutes of the meeting.

37. A shareholder's attendance at a meeting shall constitute a waiver of notice of such meeting, except when the shareholder objects at the beginning of the meeting.

38. Any action which may be taken at a meeting of the shareholders may be taken without a meeting or notice of meeting if authorized by a writing signed by all of the shareholders entitled to vote at a meeting for such purpose and filed with the Secretary of the corporation.

39. Unless otherwise provided by state law, any action which may be taken at any annual or special meeting of shareholders may be taken without a meeting and without prior notice if a consent in writing setting forth the action so taken shall be signed by the holders of outstanding shares having not less than the minimum number of votes that would be necessary to authorize or take such action at a meeting at which all shares entitled to vote thereon were present and voted.

40. Unless the consents of all shareholders entitled to vote have been solicited in writing, prompt notice shall be given of the taking of any other corporate action approved by shareholders without a meeting by less than unanimous written consent, to each of those shareholders entitled to vote who have not consented in writing.

41. Only persons in whose names shares entitled to vote stand on the stock records of the corporation on the day fixed by the board of directors for the determination of the

shareholders of record, shall be entitled to vote at any shareholders' meeting. The board of directors may fix a time as a record date for the determination of the shareholders entitled to notice of and to vote at any such meeting, or entitled to receive any such dividend or distribution, or any allotment, rights, or to exercise the rights in respect to any such change, conversion, or exchange of shares, In such case only shareholders of record on the date so fixed shall be entitled to notice of and to vote at such meeting, or to receive such dividends, distribution, or allotment of rights or to exercise such rights, as the case may be, notwithstanding a transfer of any share on the books of the company after any record date fixed as aforesaid.

42. Every shareholder entitled to vote for directors or on any other matter shall have the right to do so either in person or by one or more agents authorized by a proxy validly executed by the shareholder. A proxy may be executed by written authorization signed, or by electronic transmission authorized, by the shareholder or the shareholder's attorney in fact, giving the proxy holder(s) the power to vote the shareholder's shares. A proxy shall be deemed signed if the shareholder's name or other authorization is placed on the proxy (whether by manual signature, typewriting, telegraphic or electronic transmission or otherwise) by the shareholder or the shareholder's attorney in fact. A proxy may also be transmitted orally by telephone if submitted with information from which it may be determined that the proxy was authorized by the shareholder or the shareholder's attorney in fact. A validly executed proxy which does not state that it is irrevocable shall continue in full force and effect unless revoked by the person executing it, prior to the vote pursuant thereto, by a writing delivered to the corporation stating that the proxy is revoked or by a subsequent proxy executed by, or attendance at the meeting and voting in person by the person executing the proxy; provided, however, that no such proxy shall be valid after the expiration of eleven (11) months from the date of such proxy, unless otherwise provided in the proxy.

43. The President, or in the absence of the President, any Vice President, shall call the meeting of the shareholders to order, and shall act as Chairman of the meeting. In the absence of the President and all the Vice Presidents, shareholders shall appoint a Chairman at such meeting. The Secretary of the Corporation shall act as Secretary of all meetings of the shareholders, but in the absence of the Secretary at any meeting of the shareholders, the presiding officer shall appoint any person to act as such Secretary of the meeting.

Part D. Shares

44. Certificates for shares shall be of such form and device as the board of directors may designate and shall state the name of the record holder of the shares represented thereby; its number and date of issuance; the number of shares for which it is issued; a statement of the rights, privileges, preferences and restrictions, if any; a statement as to the redemption or conversion, if any; a statement of liens or restrictions upon transfer or voting, if any; and if the shares be assessable, or if assessments are collectible by personal action, a plain statement of such facts.

Form 8: Corporate Bylaws Sample (continued)

45. Upon surrender to the Secretary or transfer agent of the corporation of a certificate for shares duly endorsed or accompanied by proper evidence of succession, assignment or authority to transfer, it shall be the duty of the corporation to issue a new certificate to the person entitled thereto, cancel the old certificate, and record the transaction on its books.

46. In order that the corporation may determine the shareholders entitled to notice of any meeting or to vote or entitled to receive payment of any dividend or other distribution or allotment of any rights or entitled to exercise any rights in respect of any lawful action, the board may fix in advance, a record date, which shall not be more than sixty (60) nor less than ten (10) days prior to the date of such meeting nor more than sixty (60) days prior to any other action. If no record date is fixed:

    (a) The record date for determining shareholders entitled to notice of or to vote at a meeting of shareholders shall be at the close of the business on the business day next preceding the day on which notice is given or, if notice is waived, at close of business on the business day next preceding the day on which the meeting is held.

    (b) The record date for determining shareholders entitled to give consent to corporate action in writing without a meeting, when no prior action by the board is necessary, shall be the day on which the first written consent is given.

    (c) The record date for determining shareholders for any other purpose shall be the close of business on the day on which the board adopts the resolution relating thereto, or the sixtieth (60th) day prior to the date of such other action, whichever is later.

Part E. Miscellaneous Matters

47. The corporation may at its option, to the maximum extent permitted by law and by the articles, indemnify each of its agents against expenses, judgments, fines, settlements, and other amounts actually and reasonably incurred in connection with any proceeding arising by reason of the fact that such person is or was an agent of the corporation. For the purposes of this Section, an "agent" of the corporation includes a person who is or was a director, officer, employee or agent of another corporation, partnership, joint venture, trust or other enterprise, or was a director, officer, employee or agent of a corporation which was a predecessor corporation of the corporation or of any other enterprise at the request of such predecessor corporation.

48. The corporation shall keep at its principal executive office, or at the office of its transfer agent or registrar, if either be appointed and as determined by resolution of the board of directors, a record of its shareholders and the number and class of shares held by each shareholder.

49. The corporation shall keep at its principal executive office, or if its principal executive office is not in this state, at its principal business office in this state, the original or a copy of the bylaws amended to date, which shall be open to inspection by the shareholders at all reasonable times during office hours.

50. The board of directors, except as the bylaws otherwise provide, may authorize any officer or officers, agent or agents, to enter into any contract or execute any instrument in the name of and on behalf of the corporation, and such authority may be general or confined to specific instances; and, unless so authorized or ratified by the board of directors or within the agency power of any officer, no officer, agent or employee shall have the power or authority to bind the corporation by any contract or engagement or to pledge its credit or to render it liable for any purpose or to any amount.

51. The Chairman of the board, the President, or any Vice President, or any other person authorized by resolution of the board of directors by any of the foregoing designated officers, is authorized to vote on behalf of the corporation any and all shares of any other corporation or corporations, foreign or domestic, standing in the name of the corporation, The authority herein granted to said officers to vote or represent on behalf of the corporation any and all shares held by the corporation in any other corporation or corporations may be exercised by any such officer in person or by any person authorized to doe so by proxy duly elected by said officer.

52. These bylaws may be amended or repealed by the vote or written consent of holders of a majority of the outstanding shares entitled to vote; provided, however, that if the Articles of Incorporation of the corporation set forth the number of authorized directors of the corporation, the authorized number of directors may be changed only by an amendment of the Articles of Incorporation. Bylaws may be adopted, amended, or repealed by the board of directors.

CERTIFICATE

I, Michael Spadaccini, hereby certify that I am the Secretary of the initial meeting of [insert corporate name].

The foregoing bylaws, consisting of _____ pages, are a true and correct copy of the bylaws of the corporation.

IN WITNESS WHEREOF, I have hereunto set my hand and affixed the seal of the corporation this _____ day of _____, 2001.

_____

Michael Spadaccini

Form 9: Minutes of Organizational Meeting of the Board of Directors Sample

Minutes of First Meeting of Olde Craft, Inc. Board of Directors

The first meeting of the board of directors was held at 123 Elm Street, San Francisco on the 27th day of December, 2001 at 4:00 o'clock P.M.

Present were: John Jones, John Smith, and John Miller, constituting a quorum of the board.

Also present was Michael Spadaccini, attorney to the corporation.

John Jones acted as Chairman of the Meeting and John Miller acted as Secretary of the meeting.

The Articles of Incorporation of the Corporation were filed in the office of the secretary of state on July 31, 2001. A certified copy of the Articles of Incorporation has been inserted in the Minute Book of the Corporation.

RESOLVED FURTHER: That John Jones, named as this corporation's [initial agent for service of process/resident agent/registered agent] in the Articles of Incorporation, is hereby confirmed in such capacity.

RESOLVED FURTHER: That the corporate seal in the form, words, and figures impressed upon the last page of these minutes be, and it hereby is, adopted as the seal of the corporation.

RESOLVED FURTHER: That the form of stock certificates present to the board be, and it hereby is, approved and adopted, and the Secretary of the Corporation is directed to insert a specimen certificate in the Minute Book immediately following these minutes.

RESOLVED FURTHER: That 123 Elm Street, San Francisco, California, be, and the same hereby is, designated and fixed as the principal executive office for the transaction of the business of this corporation.

RESOLVED FURTHER: That the following persons were unanimously elected to the offices and at the annual salaries respectively set forth:

Title	Name	Salary
President/CEO	John Jones	$0
CFO/Treasurer	John Smith	$0
Secretary	John Miller	$0

RESOLVED FURTHER: That the fiscal year of this corporation shall end on December 31 of each year.

RESOLVED FURTHER: That the officers of the corporation are authorized and directed to pay the expenses of its incorporation and organization, including effecting reimbursement to any persons who have advanced funds to the corporation for such purposes and payment of any amounts remaining owing to the corporation's attorney and accountant for services in connection therewith.

RESOLVED FURTHER: That all contracts and transactions entered into on behalf of and for the benefit of this corporation, be and they hereby are accepted, adopted and ratified by this corporation; and

RESOLVED FURTHER: That this corporation save, defend, indemnify and hold harmless the persons who entered into said contracts and transactions on behalf and for the benefit of this corporation, from and against any liability or expense arising therefrom and thereunder.

RESOLVED FURTHER: That the officers of this corporation be, and they hereby are, authorized to sell and issue to the following persons the number of shares of capital stock of this corporation and for the consideration indicated opposite each name:

Name	Number of Shares	$ Per Share	Type and Amount of Consideration
John Jones	100,000	$.75	$75,000 in cash.
John Smith	100,000	$.75	$75,000 in property, specifically, the aggregate existing assets of the sole proprietorship known as Acme Iron Works, which includes, but is not limited to all tools, vehicles, good will, licenses, assets, bank accounts, cash, receivables.
John Miller	100,000	$.75	$5,000 in past services, specifically, for services rendered to the corporation in connection with its organization. $70,000 in intangible assets, specifically, a 25-year license to use the trade mark "Olde Craft" in connection with the sale of water, a copy of which license is attached.

RESOLVED FURTHER: That such shares shall be sold without the publication of any advertising or general solicitation.

RESOLVED FURTHER: That said shares shall be sold and issued only under exemption from both federal and state securities laws: the officers and directors of this corporation shall take such action as may be necessary or desirable to effect such exemption, and the corporation's shares shall be issued in accordance with the conditions thereof.

RESOLVED FURTHER: That each of the proposed issuees shall execute an investment representation with respect to the purchase of the securities of the corporation, and set forth therein their respective preexisting personal or business relationship with one or more of the corporation's directors or officers, or business or financial experience by reason of which they can reasonably by assumed to have the capacity to protect their own interests in connection with the transaction.

Form 9: Minutes of Organizational Meeting of the Board of Directors Sample
(continued)

RESOLVED: That an election [WILL/WILL NOT] be made to secure Subchapter "S" status for the corporation, and that such elected be effectuated through all appropriate filings with the US Internal Revenue Service.

Date: _____

_____

John Jones

Meeting Chairman

_____

John Miller

Meeting Secretary

Form 10: Investment Representation Letter Sample

July 31, 2001

To Whom It May Concern,

I am delivering this letter to Olde Craft, Inc. in connection with my purchase of 100,000 shares of Olde Craft, Inc. for a total sum of $75,000. I represent the following:

I am purchasing the shares in my own name and for my own account, for investment and not with an intent to sell, or for sale in connection with any distribution of such stock; and no other person has any interest in or right with respect to the shares; nor have I agreed to give any person any such interest or right in the future.

I recognize that the shares have not been registered under the Federal Securities Act of 1933, as amended, or qualified under any state securities law, and that any sale or transfer of the shares is subject to restrictions imposed by federal and state law.

I also recognize that I cannot dispose of the shares absent registration and qualification, or an available exemption from registration and qualification. I understand that no federal or state securities commission or other government body has approved of the fairness of the shares offered by the corporation and that the Commissioner has not and will not recommend or endorse the shares.

I have not seen or received any advertisement or general solicitation with respect to the sale of the shares.

I have a preexisting personal or business relationship with the Company or one or more of its officers, directors or controlling persons and I am aware of its character, and general financial and business circumstances.

I acknowledge that during the course of this transaction and before purchasing the shares I have been provided with financial and other written information about the Company. I have been given the opportunity by the Company to obtain any information and ask questions concerning the Company, the shares, and my investment that I felt necessary; and to the extent I availed myself of that opportunity, I have received satisfactory information and answers.

In reaching the decision to invest in the shares, I have carefully evaluated my financial resources and investment position and the risks associated with this investment, and I acknowledge that I am able to bear the economic risks of this investment.

_____

John Miller

Form 11: Appointment of Proxy for Annual or Special Shareholders' Meeting Sample

Appointment of Proxy for [Annual/Special] Meeting

SuperCorp, Inc.

Shareholder: John Miller

Number of Shares Held: 100,000

I, the undersigned, as record holder of the shares of stock of SuperCorp, Inc. described above, revoke any previous proxies and appoint the person whose name appears just below this paragraph as my proxy to attend the [annual/special] shareholders' meeting on _____ and any adjournment of that meeting.

THE BOARD STRONGLY RECOMMENDS THAT YOU RETURN THIS PROXY IF YOU DO NOT INTEND TO APPEAR PERSONALLY AT THE [ANNUAL/SPECIAL] SHARE-HOLDERS' MEETING.

The person I want to appoint as my proxy is: _____

The proxy holder is entitled to cast a total number of votes equal to, but not exceeding the number of shares which I would be entitle to cast if I were personally present.

I authorize my proxy holder to vote and otherwise represent my with regard to any business that may come before this meeting in the same manner and with the same effect as if I were personally present.

I MAY REVOKE THIS PROXY AT ANY TIME. THIS PROXY WILL LAPSE THREE MONTHS AFTER THE DATE OF ITS EXECUTION

ALL PROXIES MUST BE SIGNED. PLEASE SIGN EXACTLY AT YOUR NAME APPEARS ON YOUR STOCK CERTIFICATE. JOINT SHAREHOLDERS MUST EACH SIGN THIS PROXY. IF SIGNED BY AN ATTORNEY IN FACT, THE POWER OF ATTORNEY MUST BE ATTACHED.

IF YOU REQUIRE ASSISTANCE WITH THIS PROXY, PLEASE CONTACT THE CORPO-RATE SECRETARY: _____, AT (415) 555-1212.

Please sign your name below, and if you are signing for a business entity, please state your title:

DATE (IMPORTANT!): _____

_____

Name

_____

Title

Form 12: Long Form Appointment of Proxy for Annual or Special Shareholders' Meeting Sample

Appointment of Proxy for [Annual/Special] Meeting

SuperCorp, Inc.

Shareholder: John Miller

Number of Shares Held: 100,000

I, the undersigned, as record holder of the shares of stock of SuperCorp, Inc. described above, revoke any previous proxies and appoint the person whose name appears just below this paragraph in the box to the right as my proxy to attend the [annual/special] shareholders' meeting on _____ and any adjournment of that meeting.

THE BOARD STRONGLY RECOMMENDS THAT YOU RETURN THIS PROXY IF YOU DO NOT INTEND TO APPEAR PERSONALLY AT THE [ANNUAL/SPECIAL] SHAREHOLDERS' MEETING.

The person I want to appoint as my proxy is: _____

The proxy holder is entitled to cast a total number of votes equal to, but not exceeding the number of shares which I would be entitle to cast if I were personally present.

The shares represented by this proxy shall be voted in the following manner:

ACTIONS PROPOSED TO BE TAKEN

1. Shareholder John Miller has proposed a shareholder vote to remove John Jones from the board of directors.

    ☐ I want my proxy to vote FOR this proposal.

    ☐ I want my proxy to vote AGAINST this proposal.

    ☐ I withhold my proxy with respect to this specific vote.

2. Shareholder John Miller has proposed a shareholder vote to elect to make the corporation a close corporation.

    ☐ I want my proxy to vote FOR this proposal.

    ☐ I want my proxy to vote AGAINST this proposal.

    ☐ I withhold my proxy with respect to this specific vote.

3. Shareholder John Miller has proposed that in the event that John Jones is removed from the board of directors, that he, John Miller, be elected to serve on the board of directors.

    ☐ I want my proxy to vote FOR this proposal.

    ☐ I want my proxy to vote AGAINST this proposal.

    ☐ I withhold my proxy with respect to this specific vote.

IF YOU DO NOT INDICATE HOW YOU DESIRE YOUR SHARES TO BE VOTED, THE PROXY HOLDER WILL HAVE COMPLETE DISCRETION IN VOTING THE SHARES ON ANY MATTER VOTED AT THE MEETING.

I MAY REVOKE THIS PROXY AT ANY TIME. THIS PROXY WILL LAPSE THREE MONTHS AFTER THE DATE OF ITS EXECUTION

ALL PROXIES MUST BE SIGNED. PLEASE SIGN EXACTLY AT YOUR NAME APPEARS ON YOUR STOCK CERTIFICATE. JOINT SHAREHOLDERS MUST EACH SIGN THIS PROXY. IF SIGNED BY AN ATTORNEY IN FACT, THE POWER OF ATTORNEY MUST BE ATTACHED.

IF YOU REQUIRE ASSISTANCE WITH THIS PROXY, PLEASE CONTACT THE CORPORATE SECRETARY: _____, AT (415) 555-1212.

Please sign your name below, and if you are signing for a business entity, please state your title:

DATE (IMPORTANT!): _____

_____

Name

_____

Title

Form 13: Call for Special Meeting of Shareholders Sample

Call for Special Meeting of Shareholders of SuperCorp, Inc.

TO: The Secretary of SuperCorp, Inc.

The party or parties whose name appears below, the holder(s) of shares entitled to cast not less than 10 percent of the votes of SuperCorp Inc., do hereby call a special meeting of the shareholders of said corporation to be held _____, (date), at _____ (time), for the purpose of considering and acting upon the following matters:

[Insert matters to be considered, such as "A proposal that John Jones be removed from the board of directors."]

You are directed to give notice of this special meeting, in the manner prescribed by the corporation's bylaws and by law to all shareholders entitled to receive notice of the meeting.

Date: _____

_____

_____

_____

Form 14: Notice of Special Meeting of Shareholders Sample

Notice of Special Meeting of Shareholders of SuperCorp, Inc.

Pursuant to a call made by shareholders, notice is hereby given that a special meeting of the Shareholders of SuperCorp, Inc. be held at _____ (time), on _____, (date), at _____ (address), to consider and act on the following:

[Insert matters to be considered, such as "A proposal that John Jones be removed from the board of directors."]

If you do not expect to be present at the meeting and wish your shares to be voted, you may complete the attached form of proxy and mail it in the enclosed addressed envelope.

Date: _____

_____

Corporate Secretary

Form 15: Minutes of Annual or Special Meeting of Shareholders Sample

Minutes of (Annual/Special) Meeting of Shareholders of SuperCorp, Inc.

The shareholders of SUPERCORP, INC., held a (special/annual) meeting on _____ (date), at _____(time), at _____(place).

The following shareholders were present at the meeting, in person or by proxy, representing shares as indicated:

John Jones, 100,000 shares

John Smith, 100,000 shares

John Miller, 75,000 shares

Also present were Michael D. Spadaccini, attorney to the corporation, and Lisa Jones.

The (president, chairman of the board, secretary, etc.) of the corporation called the meeting to order and announced that she would chair the meeting, and that a quorum was present and that the meeting was held pursuant to a written notice of meeting given to all shareholders of the corporation. A copy of this notice was ordered inserted in the minute book immediately preceding the minutes of this meeting.

The minutes of the previous meeting of shareholders were then read and approved.

The chairperson then announced that the election of directors was in order. Directors were then elected to serve until the next annual meeting of stockholders, and until their successors were duly elected and qualified, as follows:

John Jones

John Smith

John Miller

The chairperson then announced a proposal to change the corporation's fiscal year from December 31 to June 30. This proposal did not receive an adequate vote for passage.

There being no further business to come before the meeting, on motion duly made, seconded, and adopted, the meeting was adjourned.

_____

Corporate Secretary

Form 16: Action By Written Consent of Shareholders Sample

Action By Written Consent of Shareholder(s) of SuperCorp, Inc.

The undersigned shareholder(s) of SuperCorp, Inc., owning of record the number of shares entitled to vote as set forth, hereby consent(s) to the following corporate actions:

1. John Smith is hereby elected to serve on the board of directors and to occupy the vacancy left by the resignation of John Jones. He shall serve until the next annual meeting of shareholders.

2. The corporation hereby elects to be a close corporation.

3. The articles of incorporation shall be amended to include language sufficient to make the close corporation election under state law.

DATED: _____

_____

John Smith

Number of Shares Owned: _____

DATED: _____

_____

John Miller

Number of Shares Owned: _____

Form 17: Call for Special Meeting of Directors Sample

Call for Special Meeting of Directors of SuperCorp, Inc.

TO: The Secretary of SuperCorp, Inc.

The party whose name appears below, the (director/CEO/president), by this notice hereby calls a special meeting of directors which shall be held on _____(date) at _____ (time), at _____ (place), to consider and act on the following proposals and such other business as may properly come before the board.

1. Acceptance of resignation of John Jones as corporate secretary.

2. Appointment of John Miller to position of corporate secretary.

3. Consideration of acquisition of NewCorp, Inc. by SuperCorp, Inc.

You are directed to give notice of this special meeting, in the manner prescribed by the corporation's bylaws and by law to all shareholders entitled to receive notice of the meeting.

Date: _____

_____

Name

_____

Position (i.e., director, CEO, President)

Form 18: Notice of Special Meeting of Board of Directors Sample

Notice of Special Meeting of the Directors of SuperCorp, Inc.

Notice is hereby given that the Chief Executive Officer of SuperCorp, Inc. has called a special meeting of the directors of SuperCorp, Inc., which shall be held on _____(date) at _____ (time), at _____ (place), to consider and act on the following proposals and such other business as may properly come before the board.

1. Acceptance of resignation of John Jones as corporate secretary.

2. Appointment of John Miller to position of corporate secretary.

3. Consideration of acquisition of NewCorp, Inc. by SuperCorp, Inc.

DATED: _____

_____

John Jones

Corporate Secretary

Form 19: Minutes of Annual Meeting of Directors Sample

Minutes of Annual Meeting of the Directors of SuperCorp, Inc.

The directors of SuperCorp, Inc. held an annual meeting at _____ (time), on _____ (date), at _____ (place) _____.

The following directors were present at the meeting:

John Jones

John Smith

John Miller

Also present were Michael D. Spadaccini, attorney to the corporation, and Lisa Jones.

The chairman called the meeting to order and announced that the meeting was held pursuant to the bylaws of the corporation, and was held without notice.

It was then moved, seconded, and resolved to dispense with the reading of the minutes of the last meeting.

The directors considered the election of officers to serve until the next annual meeting of directors. The directors unanimously voted to elect the following persons to the corresponding positions:

John Jones, President and CEO

John Smith, Treasurer and CFO

John Miller, Corporate Secretary

There being no further business to come before the meeting, the meeting was duly adjourned.

_____

Corporate Secretary

Form 20: Minutes of Special Meeting of Directors Sample

Minutes of Special Meeting of the Directors of SuperCorp, Inc.

The directors of SuperCorp, Inc. held a special meeting at _____ (time), on _____ (date), at _____ (place) _____.

The following directors were present at the meeting:

John Jones

John Smith

John Miller

Also present were Michael D. Spadaccini, attorney to the corporation, and Lisa Jones.

The chairman called the meeting to order and announced that the meeting was held pursuant to written waiver of notice and consent to the holding of the meeting. The waiver and consent was presented to the meeting and, on a motion duly made, seconded, and carried, was made a part of the records and ordered inserted in the minutes book immediately preceding the records of this meeting.

It was then moved, seconded, and resolved to dispense with the reading of the minutes of the last meeting.

The directors then considered the acceptance of resignation of John Jones as corporate secretary. The directors, with John Jones abstaining from the vote, voted to accept the resignation of John Jones.

The directors then considered the appointment of John Miller to position of corporate secretary. The directors, with John Miller abstaining from the vote, voted to appoint John Miller to the position of corporate secretary.

The directors next considered the acquisition of NewCorp, Inc. by SuperCorp, Inc. The directors voted to execute an agreement of purchase of NewCorp, Inc.

There being no further business to come before the meeting, the meeting was duly adjourned.

_____

Corporate Secretary

Form 21: Action of Directors By Written Consent Sample

Action of Director[s] By Written Consent to Approve Stock Option Plan and to Issue Shares of Stock

The undersigned, the director[s] of Evolution Water Company, Inc., agree unanimously to the following:

RESOLVED, that the undersigned directors waive notice of a special meeting of directors pursuant to the Corporation's bylaws and hereby agree that the following actions and resolutions be taken by this written consent.

RESOLVED, that the "Evolution Water Company Stock Option Plan" presented to the undersigned directors, and attached to this written consent as an exhibit, is hereby adopted by the corporation.

RESOLVED FURTHER: That the officers of this corporation be, and they hereby are, authorized to sell and issue to the following persons the number of shares of capital stock of this corporation and for the consideration indicated opposite each name:

Name: John Jones

Number of Shares: 100,000

$ Per Share: $.75

Type and Amount of Consideration: $75,000 in cash

Date: _____

_____

Scott Bess, Director

_____

Brian Bess, Director

Form 22: Written Consent of Directors Approving a Certificate of Amendment of Articles of Incorporation Changing Corporation's Name Sample

Action of Director[s] By Written Consent to Approve an Amendment to Articles of Incorporation Changing Corporate Name

The undersigned, the director[s] of PlasticWorld.com, Inc., a California corporation, agree unanimously to the following:

RESOLVED, that the undersigned directors waive notice of a special meeting of directors pursuant to the Corporation's bylaws and hereby agree that the following actions and resolutions be taken by this written consent.

RESOLVED, that the Certificate of Amendment of Articles of Incorporation presented to the undersigned directors, specifically changing the name of the corporation to PlasticUniverse, Inc. be approved by the directors.

Date: _____

_____
Scott Bess, Director

_____
Brian Bess, Director

Form 23: Certificate of Amendment of Articles of Incorporation Changing Corporation's Name Sample

Certificate of Amendment of Articles of Incorporation

The undersigned certify that:

1. They are the president and secretary, respectively, of PlasticWorld.com, Inc., corporation number 10134944.

2. Article I of the Articles of Incorporation of this corporation is hereby amended to read as follows:

   The name of this Corporation is hereby changed to PlasticUniverse, Inc.

3. The foregoing Amendment of Articles of Incorporation has been duly approved by the board of directors.

4. The foregoing Amendment of Articles of Incorporation has been duly approved by the required vote of shareholders in accordance with state law. The total number of outstanding shares of the corporation is 10,000,000. The number of shares voting in favor of the amendment equaled or exceeded the vote required. The percentage vote required was more than 50 percent.

We further declare, under penalty of perjury under the laws of the State of California that the matters set forth in this certificate are true and correct of my own knowledge.

Dated: _____

_____

Scott Bess, President

_____

Brian Bess, Secretary

Form 24: Certificate of Amendment of Articles of Incorporation Electing Close Corporation Status Sample

Certificate of Amendment of Articles of Incorporation

The undersigned certify that:

1. They are the president and secretary, respectively, of Evolution Water Company, Inc., corporation number 1059964.

2. Article V of the Articles of Incorporation of this corporation is hereby added, and the Articles of Incorporation are hereby amended to read as follows:

   All of this Corporation's issued shares of all classes shall be held of record by not more than 35 persons, and this Corporation is a close corporation.

3. The foregoing Amendment of Articles of Incorporation has been duly approved by the board of directors.

4. The foregoing Amendment of Articles of Incorporation has been duly approved by the required vote of shareholders. The total number of outstanding shares of the corporation is 98,333. The vote with respect to this amendment was unanimous.

We further declare, under penalty of perjury under the laws of the State of California that the matters set forth in this certificate are true and correct of my own knowledge.

Dated: _____

_____

Donald LeBuhn, President

_____

Alexandra LeBuhn, Secretary

Form 25: IRS Tax Form SS-4 – Application for Employer Identification Number

Form **SS-4**	**Application for Employer Identification Number**		EIN	
(Rev. April 2000)	**(For use by employers, corporations, partnerships, trusts, estates, churches, government agencies, certain individuals, and others. See instructions.)**			
Department of the Treasury Internal Revenue Service	▶ **Keep a copy for your records.**		OMB No. 1545-0003	

Please type or print clearly.

1 Name of applicant (legal name) (see instructions)

2 Trade name of business (if different from name on line 1) | **3** Executor, trustee, "care of" name

4a Mailing address (street address) (room, apt., or suite no.) | **5a** Business address (if different from address on lines 4a and 4b)

4b City, state, and ZIP code | **5b** City, state, and ZIP code

6 County and state where principal business is located

7 Name of principal officer, general partner, grantor, owner, or trustor—SSN or ITIN may be required (see instructions) ▶

8a Type of entity (Check only one box.) (see instructions)

Caution: *If applicant is a limited liability company, see the instructions for line 8a.*

☐ Sole proprietor (SSN) _____   ☐ Estate (SSN of decedent) _____
☐ Partnership   ☐ Personal service corp.   ☐ Plan administrator (SSN) _____
☐ REMIC   ☐ National Guard   ☐ Other corporation (specify) ▶ _____
☐ State/local government   ☐ Farmers' cooperative   ☐ Trust
☐ Church or church-controlled organization   ☐ Federal government/military
☐ Other nonprofit organization (specify) ▶ _____ (enter GEN if applicable) _____
☐ Other (specify) ▶

8b If a corporation, name the state or foreign country (if applicable) where incorporated | State | Foreign country

9 Reason for applying (Check only one box.) (see instructions)
☐ Started new business (specify type) ▶_____
☐ Banking purpose (specify purpose) ▶ _____
☐ Changed type of organization (specify new type) ▶ _____
☐ Purchased going business
☐ Hired employees (Check the box and see line 12.)
☐ Created a trust (specify type) ▶ _____
☐ Created a pension plan (specify type) ▶
☐ Other (specify) ▶

10 Date business started or acquired (month, day, year) (see instructions) | **11** Closing month of accounting year (see instructions)

12 First date wages or annuities were paid or will be paid (month, day, year). **Note:** *If applicant is a withholding agent, enter date income will first be paid to nonresident alien. (month, day, year)* . . . . ▶

13 Highest number of employees expected in the next 12 months. **Note:** *If the applicant does not expect to have any employees during the period, enter -0-. (see instructions)* . . . . ▶ | Nonagricultural | Agricultural | Household

14 Principal activity (see instructions) ▶

15 Is the principal business activity manufacturing? . . . . ☐ **Yes** ☐ **No**
If "Yes," principal product and raw material used ▶

16 To whom are most of the products or services sold? Please check one box.   ☐ Business (wholesale)
☐ Public (retail)   ☐ Other (specify) ▶   ☐ N/A

17a Has the applicant ever applied for an employer identification number for this or any other business? . . . . ☐ **Yes** ☐ **No**
Note: *If "Yes," please complete lines 17b and 17c.*

17b If you checked "Yes" on line 17a, give applicant's legal name and trade name shown on prior application, if different from line 1 or 2 above.
Legal name ▶   Trade name ▶

17c Approximate date when and city and state where the application was filed. Enter previous employer identification number if known.
Approximate date when filed (mo., day, year) | City and state where filed | Previous EIN

Under penalties of perjury, I declare that I have examined this application, and to the best of my knowledge and belief, it is true, correct, and complete. | Business telephone number (include area code) ( )

   | Fax telephone number (include area code) ( )

Name and title (Please type or print clearly.) ▶

Signature ▶   Date ▶

Note: *Do not write below this line. For official use only.*

Please leave blank ▶	Geo.	Ind.	Class	Size	Reason for applying

For Privacy Act and Paperwork Reduction Act Notice, see page 4.   Cat. No. 16055N   Form **SS-4** (Rev. 4-2000)

Form 25: IRS Tax Form SS-4 – Instructions

Form SS-4 (Rev. 4-2000)   Page **2**

General Instructions

Section references are to the Internal Revenue Code unless otherwise noted.

Purpose of Form

Use Form SS-4 to apply for an employer identification number (EIN). An EIN is a nine-digit number (for example, 12-3456789) assigned to sole proprietors, corporations, partnerships, estates, trusts, and other entities for tax filing and reporting purposes. The information you provide on this form will establish your business tax account.

Caution: *An EIN is for use in connection with your business activities only. Do **not** use your EIN in place of your social security number (SSN).*

Who Must File

You must file this form if you have not been assigned an EIN before and:
- You pay wages to one or more employees including household employees.
- You are required to have an EIN to use on any return, statement, or other document, even if you are not an employer.
- You are a withholding agent required to withhold taxes on income, other than wages, paid to a nonresident alien (individual, corporation, partnership, etc.). A withholding agent may be an agent, broker, fiduciary, manager, tenant, or spouse, and is required to file **Form 1042,** Annual Withholding Tax Return for U.S. Source Income of Foreign Persons.
- You file **Schedule C,** Profit or Loss From Business, **Schedule C-EZ,** Net Profit From Business, or **Schedule F,** Profit or Loss From Farming, of **Form 1040,** U.S. Individual Income Tax Return, **and** have a Keogh plan or are required to file excise, employment, or alcohol, tobacco, or firearms returns.

The following must use EINs even if they do not have any employees:
- State and local agencies who serve as tax reporting agents for public assistance recipients, under Rev. Proc. 80-4, 1980-1 C.B. 581, should obtain a separate EIN for this reporting. See **Household employer** on page 3.
- Trusts, except the following:
  1. Certain grantor-owned trusts. (See the **Instructions for Form 1041,** U.S. Income Tax Return for Estates and Trusts.)
  2. Individual retirement arrangement (IRA) trusts, unless the trust has to file **Form 990-T,** Exempt Organization Business Income Tax Return. (See the **Instructions for Form 990-T.**)
- Estates
- Partnerships
- REMICs (real estate mortgage investment conduits) (See the **Instructions for Form 1066,** U.S. Real Estate Mortgage Investment Conduit (REMIC) Income Tax Return.)
- Corporations
- Nonprofit organizations (churches, clubs, etc.)
- Farmers' cooperatives
- Plan administrators (A plan administrator is the person or group of persons specified as the administrator by the instrument under which the plan is operated.)

When To Apply for a New EIN

New Business. If you become the new owner of an existing business, **do not** use the EIN of the former owner. **If you already have an EIN, use that number.** If you do not have an EIN, apply for one on this form. If you become the "owner" of a corporation by acquiring its stock, use the corporation's EIN.

Changes in Organization or Ownership. If you already have an EIN, you may need to get a new one if either the organization or ownership of your business changes. If you incorporate a sole proprietorship or form a partnership, you must get a new EIN. However, **do not** apply for a new EIN if:
- You change only the name of your business,
- You elected on **Form 8832,** Entity Classification Election, to change the way the entity is taxed, or
- A partnership terminates because at least 50% of the total interests in partnership capital and profits were sold or exchanged within a 12-month period. (See Regulations section 301.6109-1(d)(2)(iii).) The EIN for the terminated partnership should continue to be used.

Note: *If you are electing to be an "S corporation," be sure you file **Form 2553,** Election by a Small Business Corporation.*

File Only One Form SS-4. File only one Form SS-4, regardless of the number of businesses operated or trade names under which a business operates. However, each corporation in an affiliated group must file a separate application.

EIN Applied for, But Not Received. If you do not have an EIN by the time a return is due, write "Applied for" and the date you applied in the space shown for the number. **Do not** show your social security number (SSN) as an EIN on returns.

If you do not have an EIN by the time a tax deposit is due, send your payment to the Internal Revenue Service Center for your filing area. (See **Where To Apply** below.) Make your check or money order payable to "United States Treasury" and show your name (as shown on Form SS-4), address, type of tax, period covered, and date you applied for an EIN. Send an explanation with the deposit.

For more information about EINs, see **Pub. 583,** Starting a Business and Keeping Records, and **Pub. 1635,** Understanding Your EIN.

How To Apply

You can apply for an EIN either by mail or by telephone. You can get an EIN immediately by calling the Tele-TIN number for the service center for your state, or you can send the completed Form SS-4 directly to the service center to receive your EIN by mail.

Application by Tele-TIN. Under the Tele-TIN program, you can receive your EIN by telephone and use it immediately to file a return or make a payment. To receive an EIN by telephone, complete Form SS-4, then call the Tele-TIN number listed for your state under **Where To Apply.** The person making the call must be authorized to sign the form. (See **Signature** on page 4.)

An IRS representative will use the information from the Form SS-4 to establish your account and assign you an EIN. Write the number you are given on the upper right corner of the form and sign and date it.

*Mail or fax (facsimile) the signed Form SS-4 **within 24 hours** to the Tele-TIN Unit at the service center address for your state.* The IRS representative will give you the fax number. The fax numbers are also listed in Pub. 1635.

Taxpayer representatives can receive their client's EIN by telephone if they first send a fax of a completed **Form 2848,** Power of Attorney and Declaration of Representative, or **Form 8821,** Tax Information Authorization, to the Tele-TIN unit. The Form 2848 or Form 8821 will be used solely to release the EIN to the representative authorized on the form.

Application by Mail. Complete Form SS-4 at least 4 to 5 weeks before you will need an EIN. Sign and date the application and mail it to the service center address for your state. You will receive your EIN in the mail in approximately 4 weeks.

Where To Apply

The Tele-TIN numbers listed below will involve a long-distance charge to callers outside of the local calling area and can be used only to apply for an EIN. **The numbers may change without notice.** Call 1-800-829-1040 to verify a number or to ask about the status of an application by mail.

If your principal business, office or agency, or legal residence in the case of an individual, is located in:	Call the Tele-TIN number shown or file with the Internal Revenue Service Center at:
Florida, Georgia, South Carolina	Attn: Entity Control Atlanta, GA 39901 770-455-2360
New Jersey, New York (New York City and counties of Nassau, Rockland, Suffolk, and Westchester)	Attn: Entity Control Holtsville, NY 00501 516-447-4955
New York (all other counties), Connecticut, Maine, Massachusetts, New Hampshire, Rhode Island, Vermont	Attn: Entity Control Andover, MA 05501 978-474-9717
Illinois, Iowa, Minnesota, Missouri, Wisconsin	Attn: Entity Control Stop 6800 2306 E. Bannister Rd. Kansas City, MO 64999 816-926-5999
Delaware, District of Columbia, Maryland, Pennsylvania, Virginia	Attn: Entity Control Philadelphia, PA 19255 215-516-6999
Indiana, Kentucky, Michigan, Ohio, West Virginia	Attn: Entity Control Cincinnati, OH 45999 859-292-5467

Form 25: IRS Tax Form SS-4 – Instructions

Form SS-4 (Rev. 4-2000)   Page **3**

Kansas, New Mexico, Oklahoma, Texas	Attn: Entity Control Austin, TX 73301 512-460-7843
Alaska, Arizona, California (counties of Alpine, Amador, Butte, Calaveras, Colusa, Contra Costa, Del Norte, El Dorado, Glenn, Humboldt, Lake, Lassen, Marin, Mendocino, Modoc, Napa, Nevada, Placer, Plumas, Sacramento, San Joaquin, Shasta, Sierra, Siskiyou, Solano, Sonoma, Sutter, Tehama, Trinity, Yolo, and Yuba), Colorado, Idaho, Montana, Nebraska, Nevada, North Dakota, Oregon, South Dakota, Utah, Washington, Wyoming	Attn: Entity Control Mail Stop 6271 P.O. Box 9941 Ogden, UT 84201 801-620-7645
California (all other counties), Hawaii	Attn: Entity Control Fresno, CA 93888 559-452-4010
Alabama, Arkansas, Louisiana, Mississippi, North Carolina, Tennessee	Attn: Entity Control Memphis, TN 37501 901-546-3920
If you have no legal residence, principal place of business, or principal office or agency in any state	Attn: Entity Control Philadelphia, PA 19255 215-516-6999

Specific Instructions

The instructions that follow are for those items that are not self-explanatory. Enter N/A (nonapplicable) on the lines that do not apply.

Line 1. Enter the legal name of the entity applying for the EIN exactly as it appears on the social security card, charter, or other applicable legal document.

Individuals. Enter your first name, middle initial, and last name. If you are a sole proprietor, enter your individual name, not your business name. Enter your business name on line 2. Do not use abbreviations or nicknames on line 1.

Trusts. Enter the name of the trust.

Estate of a decedent. Enter the name of the estate.

Partnerships. Enter the legal name of the partnership as it appears in the partnership agreement. **Do not** list the names of the partners on line 1. See the specific instructions for line 7.

Corporations. Enter the corporate name as it appears in the corporation charter or other legal document creating it.

Plan administrators. Enter the name of the plan administrator. A plan administrator who already has an EIN should use that number.

Line 2. Enter the trade name of the business if different from the legal name. The trade name is the "doing business as" name.

Note: *Use the full legal name on line 1 on all tax returns filed for the entity. However, if you enter a trade name on line 2 and choose to use the trade name instead of the legal name, enter the trade name on all returns you file. To prevent processing delays and errors, **always** use either the legal name only or the trade name only on all tax returns.*

Line 3. Trusts enter the name of the trustee. Estates enter the name of the executor, administrator, or other fiduciary. If the entity applying has a designated person to receive tax information, enter that person's name as the "care of" person. Print or type the first name, middle initial, and last name.

Line 7. Enter the first name, middle initial, last name, and SSN of a principal officer if the business is a corporation; of a general partner if a partnership; of the owner of a single member entity that is disregarded as an entity separate from its owner; or of a grantor, owner, or trustor if a trust. If the person in question is an alien individual with a previously assigned individual taxpayer identification number (ITIN), enter the ITIN in the space provided, instead of an SSN. You are not required to enter an SSN or ITIN if the reason you are applying for an EIN is to make an entity classification election (see Regulations section 301.7701-1 through 301.7701-3), and you are a nonresident alien with no effectively connected income from sources within the United States.

Line 8a. Check the box that best describes the type of entity applying for the EIN. If you are an alien individual with an ITIN previously assigned to you, enter the ITIN in place of a requested SSN.

Caution: *This is not an election for a tax classification of an entity. See "Limited liability company (LLC)" below.*

If not specifically mentioned, check the "Other" box, enter the type of entity and the type of return that will be filed (for example, common trust fund, Form 1065). Do not enter N/A. If you are an alien individual applying for an EIN, see the **Line 7** instructions above.

Sole proprietor. Check this box if you file Schedule C, C-EZ, or F (Form 1040) and have a qualified plan, or are required to file excise, employment, or alcohol, tobacco, or firearms returns, or are a payer of gambling winnings. Enter your SSN (or ITIN) in the space provided. If you are a nonresident alien with are a nonresident alien with no effectively

connected income from sources within the United States, you do not need to enter an SSN or ITIN.

REMIC. Check this box if the entity has elected to be treated as a real estate mortgage investment conduit (REMIC). See the Instructions for Form 1066 for more information.

Other nonprofit organization. Check this box if the nonprofit organization is other than a church or church-controlled organization and specify the type of nonprofit organization (for example, an educational organization).

If the organization also seeks tax-exempt status, you must file either **Package 1023,** Application for Recognition of Exemption, or **Package 1024,** Application for Recognition of Exemption Under Section 501(a). Get **Pub. 557,** Tax Exempt Status for Your Organization, for more information.

Group exemption number (GEN). If the organization is covered by a group exemption letter, enter the four-digit GEN. (Do not confuse the GEN with the nine-digit EIN.) If you do not know the GEN, contact the parent organization. Get Pub. 557 for more information about group exemption numbers.

Withholding agent. If you are a withholding agent required to file Form 1042, check the "Other" box and enter "Withholding agent."

Personal service corporation. Check this box if the entity is a personal service corporation. An entity is a personal service corporation for a tax year only if:

● The principal activity of the entity during the testing period (prior tax year) for the tax year is the performance of personal services substantially by employee-owners, and

● The employee-owners own at least 10% of the fair market value of the outstanding stock in the entity on the last day of the testing period.

Personal services include performance of services in such fields as health, law, accounting, or consulting. For more information about personal service corporations, see the **Instructions for Forms 1120 and 1120-A,** and **Pub. 542,** Corporations.

Limited liability company (LLC). See the definition of limited liability company in the **Instructions for Form 1065,** U.S. Partnership Return of Income. An LLC with two or more members can be a partnership or an association taxable as a corporation. An LLC with a single owner can be an association taxable as a corporation or an entity disregarded as an entity separate from its owner. See Form 8832 for more details.

Note: *A domestic LLC with at least two members that does not file Form 8832 is classified as a partnership for Federal income tax purposes.*

● If the entity is classified as a partnership for Federal income tax purposes, check the "partnership" box.

● If the entity is classified as a corporation for Federal income tax purposes, check the "Other corporation" box and write "limited liability co." in the space provided.

● If the entity is disregarded as an entity separate from its owner, check the "Other" box and write in "disregarded entity" in the space provided.

Plan administrator. If the plan administrator is an individual, enter the plan administrator's SSN in the space provided.

Other corporation. This box is for any corporation other than a personal service corporation. If you check this box, enter the type of corporation (such as insurance company) in the space provided.

Household employer. If you are an individual, check the "Other" box and enter "Household employer" and your SSN. If you are a state or local agency serving as a tax reporting agent for public assistance recipients who become household employers, check the "Other" box and enter "Household employer agent." If you are a trust that qualifies as a household employer, you do not need a separate EIN for reporting tax information relating to household employees; use the EIN of the trust.

QSub. For a qualified subchapter S subsidiary (QSub) check the "Other" box and specify "QSub."

Line 9. Check only **one** box. Do not enter N/A.

Started new business. Check this box if you are starting a new business that requires an EIN. If you check this box, enter the type of business being started. **Do not** apply if you already have an EIN and are only adding another place of business.

Hired employees. Check this box if the existing business is requesting an EIN because it has hired or is hiring employees and is therefore required to file employment tax returns. **Do not** apply if you already have an EIN and are only hiring employees. For information on the applicable employment taxes for family members, see **Circular E,** Employer's Tax Guide (Publication 15).

Created a pension plan. Check this box if you have created a pension plan and need an EIN for reporting purposes. Also, enter the type of plan.

Note: *Check this box if you are applying for a trust EIN when a new pension plan is established.*

Form 25: IRS Tax Form SS-4 – Instructions

Form SS-4 (Rev. 4-2000)   Page **4**

Banking purpose. Check this box if you are requesting an EIN for banking purposes only, and enter the banking purpose (for example, a bowling league for depositing dues or an investment club for dividend and interest reporting).

Changed type of organization. Check this box if the business is changing its type of organization, for example, if the business was a sole proprietorship and has been incorporated or has become a partnership. If you check this box, specify in the space provided the type of change made, for example, "from sole proprietorship to partnership."

Purchased going business. Check this box if you purchased an existing business. **Do not** use the former owner's EIN. **Do not** apply for a new EIN if you already have one. Use your own EIN.

Created a trust. Check this box if you created a trust, and enter the type of trust created. For example, indicate if the trust is a nonexempt charitable trust or a split-interest trust.

Note: **Do not** *check this box if you are applying for a trust EIN when a new pension plan is established. Check "Created a pension plan."*

Exception. Do **not** file this form for certain grantor-type trusts. The trustee does not need an EIN for the trust if the trustee furnishes the name and TIN of the grantor/owner and the address of the trust to all payors. See the Instructions for Form 1041 for more information.

Other (specify). Check this box if you are requesting an EIN for any other reason, and enter the reason.

Line 10. If you are starting a new business, enter the starting date of the business. If the business you acquired is already operating, enter the date you acquired the business. Trusts should enter the date the trust was legally created. Estates should enter the date of death of the decedent whose name appears on line 1 or the date when the estate was legally funded.

Line 11. Enter the last month of your accounting year or tax year. An accounting or tax year is usually 12 consecutive months, either a calendar year or a fiscal year (including a period of 52 or 53 weeks). A calendar year is 12 consecutive months ending on December 31. A fiscal year is either 12 consecutive months ending on the last day of any month other than December or a 52-53 week year. For more information on accounting periods, see **Pub. 538,** Accounting Periods and Methods.

Individuals. Your tax year generally will be a calendar year.

Partnerships. Partnerships generally must adopt one of the following tax years:
● The tax year of the majority of its partners,
● The tax year common to all of its principal partners,
● The tax year that results in the least aggregate deferral of income, or
● In certain cases, some other tax year.
See the Instructions for Form 1065 for more information.

REMIC. REMICs must have a calendar year as their tax year.

Personal service corporations. A personal service corporation generally must adopt a calendar year unless:
● It can establish a business purpose for having a different tax year, or
● It elects under section 444 to have a tax year other than a calendar year.

Trusts. Generally, a trust must adopt a calendar year except for the following:
● Tax-exempt trusts,
● Charitable trusts, and
● Grantor-owned trusts.

Line 12. If the business has or will have employees, enter the date on which the business began or will begin to pay wages. If the business does not plan to have employees, enter N/A.

Withholding agent. Enter the date you began or will begin to pay income to a nonresident alien. This also applies to individuals who are required to file Form 1042 to report alimony paid to a nonresident alien.

Line 13. For a definition of agricultural labor (farmwork), see **Circular A,** Agricultural Employer's Tax Guide (Publication 51).

Line 14. Generally, enter the exact type of business being operated (for example, advertising agency, farm, food or beverage establishment, labor union, real estate agency, steam laundry, rental of coin-operated vending machine, or investment club). Also state if the business will involve the sale or distribution of alcoholic beverages.

Governmental. Enter the type of organization (state, county, school district, municipality, etc.).

Nonprofit organization (other than governmental). Enter whether organized for religious, educational, or humane purposes, and the principal activity (for example, religious organization—hospital, charitable).

Mining and quarrying. Specify the process and the principal product (for example, mining bituminous coal, contract drilling for oil, or quarrying dimension stone).

Contract construction. Specify whether general contracting or special trade contracting. Also, show the type of work normally performed (for example, general contractor for residential buildings or electrical subcontractor).

Food or beverage establishments. Specify the type of establishment and state whether you employ workers who receive tips (for example, lounge—yes).

Trade. Specify the type of sales and the principal line of goods sold (for example, wholesale dairy products, manufacturer's representative for mining machinery, or retail hardware).

Manufacturing. Specify the type of establishment operated (for example, sawmill or vegetable cannery).

Signature. The application must be signed by (a) the individual, if the applicant is an individual, (b) the president, vice president, or other principal officer, if the applicant is a corporation, (c) a responsible and duly authorized member or officer having knowledge of its affairs, if the applicant is a partnership or other unincorporated organization, or (d) the fiduciary, if the applicant is a trust or an estate.

How To Get Forms and Publications

Phone. You can order forms, instructions, and publications by phone 24 hours a day, 7 days a week. Just call 1-800-TAX-FORM (1-800-829-3676). You should receive your order or notification of its status within 10 workdays.

Personal computer. With your personal computer and modem, you can get the forms and information you need using IRS's Internet Web Site at **www.irs.gov** or File Transfer Protocol at **ftp.irs.gov.**

CD-ROM. For small businesses, return preparers, or others who may frequently need tax forms or publications, a CD-ROM containing over 2,000 tax products (including many prior year forms) can be purchased from the National Technical Information Service (NTIS).

To order **Pub. 1796,** Federal Tax Products on CD-ROM, call **1-877-CDFORMS** (1-877-233-6767) toll free or connect to **www.irs.gov/cdorders**

Privacy Act and Paperwork Reduction Act Notice. We ask for the information on this form to carry out the Internal Revenue laws of the United States. We need it to comply with section 6109 and the regulations thereunder which generally require the inclusion of an employer identification number (EIN) on certain returns, statements, or other documents filed with the Internal Revenue Service. Information on this form may be used to determine which Federal tax returns you are required to file and to provide you with related forms and publications. We disclose this form to the Social Security Administration for their use in determining compliance with applicable laws. We will be unable to issue an EIN to you unless you provide all of the requested information which applies to your entity.

You are not required to provide the information requested on a form that is subject to the Paperwork Reduction Act unless the form displays a valid OMB control number. Books or records relating to a form or its instructions must be retained as long as their contents may become material in the administration of any Internal Revenue law. Generally, tax returns/return information are confidential, as required by section 6103.

The time needed to complete and file this form will vary depending on individual circumstances. The estimated average time is:

Recordkeeping	7 min.
Learning about the law or the form	22 min.
Preparing the form	46 min.
Copying, assembling, and sending the form to the IRS . .	20 min.

If you have comments concerning the accuracy of these time estimates or suggestions for making this form simpler, we would be happy to hear from you. You can write to the Tax Forms Committee, Western Area Distribution Center, Rancho Cordova, CA 95743-0001. **Do not** send the form to this address. Instead, see **Where To Apply** on page 2.

Form 26: IRS Tax Form 2553 – Election by a Small Business Corporation

Form **2553** (Rev. July 1999) Department of the Treasury Internal Revenue Service	**Election by a Small Business Corporation** (Under section 1362 of the Internal Revenue Code) ▶ See Parts II and III on back and the separate instructions. ▶ The corporation may either send or fax this form to the IRS. See page 1 of the instructions.	OMB No. 1545-0146

Notes: **1.** *This election to be an S corporation can be accepted only if all the tests are met under **Who may elect** on page 1 of the instructions; all signatures in Parts I and III are originals (no photocopies); and the exact name and address of the corporation and other required form information are provided.*

2. *Do not file **Form 1120S**, U.S. Income Tax Return for an S Corporation, for any tax year before the year the election takes effect.*

3. *If the corporation was in existence before the effective date of this election, see **Taxes an S corporation may owe** on page 1 of the instructions.*

Election Information

Please Type or Print	Name of corporation (see instructions)	**A** Employer identification number
	Number, street, and room or suite no. (If a P.O. box, see instructions.)	**B** Date incorporated
	City or town, state, and ZIP code	**C** State of incorporation

D Election is to be effective for tax year beginning (month, day, year) . . . . ▶   /   /

E Name and title of officer or legal representative who the IRS may call for more information

F Telephone number of officer or legal representative (   )

G If the corporation changed its name or address after applying for the EIN shown in **A** above, check this box . . . . ▶ ☐

H If this election takes effect for the first tax year the corporation exists, enter month, day, and year of the **earliest** of the following: (1) date the corporation first had shareholders, (2) date the corporation first had assets, or (3) date the corporation began doing business . . . . ▶   /   /

I Selected tax year: Annual return will be filed for tax year ending (month and day) ▶ ....

If the tax year ends on any date other than December 31, except for an automatic 52-53-week tax year ending with reference to the month of December, you **must** complete Part II on the back. If the date you enter is the ending date of an automatic 52-53-week tax year, write "52-53-week year" to the right of the date. See Temporary Regulations section 1.441-2T(e)(3).

J Name and address of each shareholder; shareholder's spouse having a community property interest in the corporation's stock; and each tenant in common, joint tenant, and tenant by the entirety. (A husband and wife (and their estates) are counted as one shareholder in determining the number of shareholders without regard to the manner in which the stock is owned.)	**K** Shareholders' Consent Statement. Under penalties of perjury, we declare that we consent to the election of the above-named corporation to be an S corporation under section 1362(a) and that we have examined this consent statement, including accompanying schedules and statements, and to the best of our knowledge and belief, it is true, correct, and complete. We understand our consent is binding and may not be withdrawn after the corporation has made a valid election. (Shareholders sign and date below.)		**L** Stock owned		**M** Social security number or employer identification number (see instructions)	**N** Share-holder's tax year ends (month and day)
	Signature	Date	Number of shares	Dates acquired		

Under penalties of perjury, I declare that I have examined this election, including accompanying schedules and statements, and to the best of my knowledge and belief, it is true, correct, and complete.

Signature of officer ▶   Title ▶   Date ▶

For Paperwork Reduction Act Notice, see page 2 of the instructions.   Cat. No. 18629R   Form **2553** (Rev. 7-99)

Form 26: IRS Tax Form 2553 – Election by a Small Business Corporation

Form 2553 (Rev. 7-99)   Page **2**

      Selection of Fiscal Tax Year (All corporations using this part must complete item O and item P, Q, or R.)

O　Check the applicable box to indicate whether the corporation is:

  1.　☐　A new corporation adopting the tax year entered in item I, Part I.

  2.　☐　An existing corporation retaining the tax year entered in item I, Part I.

  3.　☐　An existing corporation changing to the tax year entered in item I, Part I.

P　Complete item P if the corporation is using the expeditious approval provisions of Rev. Proc. 87-32, 1987-2 C.B. 396, to request **(1)** a natural business year (as defined in section 4.01(1) of Rev. Proc. 87-32) or **(2)** a year that satisfies the ownership tax year test in section 4.01(2) of Rev. Proc. 87-32. Check the applicable box below to indicate the representation statement the corporation is making as required under section 4 of Rev. Proc. 87-32.

  1. Natural Business Year ▶ ☐ I represent that the corporation is retaining or changing to a tax year that coincides with its natural business year as defined in section 4.01(1) of Rev. Proc. 87-32 and as verified by its satisfaction of the requirements of section 4.02(1) of Rev. Proc. 87-32. In addition, if the corporation is changing to a natural business year as defined in section 4.01(1), I further represent that such tax year results in less deferral of income to the owners than the corporation's present tax year. I also represent that the corporation is not described in section 3.01(2) of Rev. Proc. 87-32. (See instructions for additional information that must be attached.)

  2. Ownership Tax Year ▶ ☐ I represent that shareholders holding more than half of the shares of the stock (as of the first day of the tax year to which the request relates) of the corporation have the same tax year or are concurrently changing to the tax year that the corporation adopts, retains, or changes to per item I, Part I. I also represent that the corporation is not described in section 3.01(2) of Rev. Proc. 87-32.

Note: *If you do not use item P and the corporation wants a fiscal tax year, complete either item Q or R below. Item Q is used to request a fiscal tax year based on a business purpose and to make a back-up section 444 election. Item R is used to make a regular section 444 election.*

Q　Business Purpose—To request a fiscal tax year based on a business purpose, you must check box Q1 and pay a user fee. See instructions for details. You may also check box Q2 and/or box Q3.

  1. Check here ▶ ☐ if the fiscal year entered in item I, Part I, is requested under the provisions of section 6.03 of Rev. Proc. 87-32. Attach to Form 2553 a statement showing the business purpose for the requested fiscal year. See instructions for additional information that must be attached.

  2. Check here ▶ ☐ to show that the corporation intends to make a back-up section 444 election in the event the corporation's business purpose request is not approved by the IRS. (See instructions for more information.)

  3. Check here ▶ ☐ to show that the corporation agrees to adopt or change to a tax year ending December 31 if necessary for the IRS to accept this election for S corporation status in the event (1) the corporation's business purpose request is not approved and the corporation makes a back-up section 444 election, but is ultimately not qualified to make a section 444 election, or (2) the corporation's business purpose request is not approved and the corporation did not make a back-up section 444 election.

R　Section 444 Election—To make a section 444 election, you must check box R1 and you may also check box R2.

  1. Check here ▶ ☐ to show the corporation will make, if qualified, a section 444 election to have the fiscal tax year shown in item I, Part I. To make the election, you must complete **Form 8716,** Election To Have a Tax Year Other Than a Required Tax Year, and either attach it to Form 2553 or file it separately.

  2. Check here ▶ ☐ to show that the corporation agrees to adopt or change to a tax year ending December 31 if necessary for the IRS to accept this election for S corporation status in the event the corporation is ultimately not qualified to make a section 444 election.

      Qualified Subchapter S Trust (QSST) Election Under Section 1361(d)(2)*

Income beneficiary's name and address	Social security number
Trust's name and address	Employer identification number

Date on which stock of the corporation was transferred to the trust (month, day, year) . . . . ▶   / /

In order for the trust named above to be a QSST and thus a qualifying shareholder of the S corporation for which this Form 2553 is filed, I hereby make the election under section 1361(d)(2). Under penalties of perjury, I certify that the trust meets the definitional requirements of section 1361(d)(3) and that all other information provided in Part III is true, correct, and complete.

_____   _____

Signature of income beneficiary or signature and title of legal representative or other qualified person making the election   Date

*Use Part III to make the QSST election only if stock of the corporation has been transferred to the trust on or before the date on which the corporation makes its election to be an S corporation. The QSST election must be made and filed separately if stock of the corporation is transferred to the trust after the date on which the corporation makes the S election.

⊛

Form **2553** (Rev. 7-99)

State Reference Tables

To help you get a better understanding of whom to contact and what to expect in a particular state when incorporating a business, this appendix offers you state-specific information and online resources. For federal corporate tax forms, go to:

Internal Revenue Service
http://www.irs.gov/plain/forms_pubs/index.html

For a convenient table with links to the secretary of states' offices for all 50 states, go to:

LearnAboutLaw.com
http://www.learnaboutlaw.com/learnaboutincorporation.htm

For a comprehensive list of links to state statutes and codes, go to:

Legal Information Institute
http://www.law.cornell.edu/topics/state_statutes.html

Please keep in mind that the information in these tables is constantly changing. Check with the secretary of state's office to confirm that the information is still current.

Alabama

Corporations Division
Alabama Secretary of State
11 South Union Street, Room 207
Montgomery, AL 36104
(334) 242-5324
http://www.sos.state.al.us/

Incorporating Fee

The fee for filing articles of incorporation is $50 payable to the Alabama Secretary of State; articles of incorporation must be filed in the county where the corporation's registered office is located. There are additional local fees payable to the probate judge and the county.

Name Reservation

For Domestic Corporations: To reserve a corporate name, call the Alabama Corporations Call Center at (334) 242-5324 or fax (334) 240-3138 your request to the Corporations Division. If the name is available, you will be issued a certificate of name reservation, and you will have 120 days to file the certificate with your articles of incorporation. If you do not incorporate within the 120 days, your name reservation will expire and you owe the Secretary of State a $10 cancellation fee for the name reservation that was issued. After 120 days, you may renew ($10) the name reservation for an additional 120 days.

For Foreign Corporations: To reserve a corporate name, you must submit an Application for Registration of Foreign Corporate Name with a fee of between $5 and $12 dollars. (See the form for an explanation.)

Corporate Forms: http://www.sos.state.al.us/business/corporations.cfm

Periodic Reporting Requirements

Alabama corporations and qualified foreign corporations must file an Alabama Business Privilege Tax Return, which also serves as an annual report. This form is due by March 15.

Corporate Taxes

Corporate Entrance Fee: Applies to foreign corporations doing business in Alabama upon entry: 25 percent of the first $100, plus 5 percent on the next $900, plus 1/10 of 1 percent of all over $1,000 of actual capital employed in Alabama during initial year of qualification.

Corporate Franchise Tax: Ruled unconstitutional in 1999.

Corporate Income Tax: Applies to net taxable income from business within the state: 5 percent of annual net income with a deduction allowed for federal income tax paid or accrued.

Corporate Permit Fee: From $5 to $100 depending on value of paid capital stock.

Tax Forms: http://www.ador.state.al.us/incometax/BPT_INDEX.htm

S Corporations

Alabama requires the filing of Form 20S to qualify as an S corporation.

Alaska

Corporations Section
Alaska Department of Community and Economic Development
P.O. Box 110808
Juneau, AK 99801-0808
(907) 465-2530
(907) 465-2549 (fax)
http://www.dced.state.ak.us/bsc/bsc.htm

The fee for filing articles of incorporation is $250. **Incorporating Fee**

Alaska incorporators may pay a $25 name reservation fee to reserve a name. The name reservation remains effective for 120 days. **Name Reservation**

Corporate Forms: http://www.dced.state.ak.us/bsc/cforms.htm. Alaska has fill-in-the-blank articles of incorporation and bylaw forms at this site.

Alaska corporations and qualified foreign corporations must file a biennial report in January of each alternate year with the Corporations Section. Visit the website to obtain a form. The biennial corporation tax is $100 for domestic corporations and $200 for foreign corporations. **Periodic Reporting Requirements**

Alaska collects an annual corporate income tax. Contact the Alaska Department of Revenue for more information. **Corporate Taxes**

Tax Forms: http://www.revenue.state.ak.us/tax/index.htm

Alaska recognizes the federal S corporation provision. The Subchapter S election is automatic and no state-specific forms need be filed to make the Subchapter S election. **S Corporations**

Arizona

Corporations Division
Arizona Corporation Commission
1300 West Washington Street
Phoenix, AZ 85007-2996
(602) 542-3026
(800) 345-5819
http://www.sosaz.com/

Incorporating Fee

The fee for filing articles of incorporation is $60. A fill-in-the-blank form is available on the Arizona Corporation Commission's website. Incorporators must publish a copy of the articles of incorporation in a newspaper of general circulation in the county of the known place of business in Arizona, for three consecutive publications. Then an Affidavit of Publication must be filed with the Arizona Corporation Commission.

Name Reservation

The Arizona Corporation Commission offers informal preliminary name availability information by telephone at (602) 542-3230. Arizona incorporators may reserve a corporate name by filing a reservation of name form with the Arizona Corporation Commission along with a $10 fee. Use the form provided on the website to reserve a name.

Corporate Forms: http://www.cc.state.az.us/corp/filings/forms/index.htm

Periodic Reporting Requirements

Arizona corporations are required to file an annual report with the Arizona Corporation Commission. The filing fee is $45. Financial disclosures are no longer required. The due date is dependent upon the first letter of the corporate name. Visit the website for a schedule of due dates.

Corporate Taxes

Arizona collects an annual corporate income tax. Contact the Arizona Department of Revenue for more information.

Tax Forms: http://www.revenue.state.az.us/

S Corporations

Arizona requires S corporations to file Form 120S annually.

Arkansas

Corporations Division
Arkansas Secretary of State
State Capitol
Little Rock, AR 72201-1094
(501) 682-3409
(888) 233-0325
http://sos.state.ar.us/

The fee for filing articles of incorporation is $50. Online filing is available at the Arkansas Secretary of State's website. **Incorporating Fee**

Arkansas incorporators may reserve a corporate name by filing a name reservation application with the Arkansas Secretary of State along with a $25 name reservation fee. The name reservation remains effective for 120 days. **Name Reservation**

Corporate Forms: http://sos.state.ar.us/corp_forms/forms.html

Arkansas corporations are required to file an Arizona Corporation Franchise Tax Report by June 1 of each year with the Arkansas Secretary of State. **Periodic Reporting Requirements**

Corporate taxes are based on total outstanding capital stock and assets in use in Arkansas. For more information, contact the Arkansas Corporate Franchise Tax Division at (501) 682-3464. **Corporate Taxes**

Tax Forms: http://sos.state.ar.us/corp_forms/forms.html

Arkansas recognizes the federal S corporation provision. The Subchapter S election is automatic and no state-specific forms need be filed to make the Subchapter S election. **S Corporations**

California

California Secretary of State
1500 11th Street
Sacramento, CA 95814
(916) 657-5448
http://www.ss.ca.gov/

Incorporating Fee

The fee for filing articles of incorporation is $100. The $800 minimum franchise tax—formerly payable upon incorporation—is now forgiven for new corporations that meet certain criteria. For new corporations that qualify or incorporate after January 1, 2000, the minimum tax is $0.00 for the first income year, measured for the second income year, and $800 for subsequent years.

Name Reservation

California incorporators may pay a $10 fee to reserve a name. The name reservation remains effective for 60 days.

Corporate Forms: http://www.ss.ca.gov/business/corp/corp_formsfees.htm

Periodic Reporting Requirements

California corporations and qualified foreign corporations must file Statement of Officers within 90 days of incorporation accompanied by a $20 fee, and biennially thereafter. Electronic filing is now available on the secretary of state's website.

Special Rules

A $250 penalty will be assessed if the annual franchise tax return is not filed within one year. Corporation status will be suspended if the $800 annual franchise tax is not filed and paid within approximately 24 to 30 months of your due date.

Corporate Taxes

California corporations and foreign corporations doing business in California are required to pay a minimum $800 annual franchise tax due within three months of the close of the accounting year, but see above under "Incorporating Fee" for first and second year exemptions. C corporations pay 8.84 percent of income.

Tax Forms: http://www.ftb.ca.gov/forms/index.htm

S Corporations

California requires the filing of Form FTP3560, S Corporation Election or Termination/Revocation, to qualify as an S corporation. S corporations pay the $800 minimum franchise tax, or 1.5 percent of income.

Colorado

Business Division
Colorado Secretary of State
1560 Broadway, Suite 200
Denver, CO 80202
(303) 894-2251
sos.admin1@state.co.us
http://www.sos.state.co.us/

The fee for filing articles of incorporation is $50.

Incorporating Fee

Colorado incorporators may check the availability of a proposed name by faxing a letter or Colorado's Form 038 to (303) 894-2242. There is a $3.00 fee for the first three names searched and a $1.00 fee for each additional name thereafter. Alternatively, incorporations may check name availability by using a 900 number service by faxing to (900) 555-1515. The same fees apply. Be sure to include your return fax on your correspondence.

Name Reservation

Corporate Forms: http://www.sos.state.co.us/pubs/info_center/main.htm

Corporate reports are due biennially by the end of the second month in which the corporate report is mailed to the corporation. The biennial fee is $25.

Periodic Reporting Requirements

Colorado corporations and foreign corporations doing business in Colorado must pay a corporate income tax. The tax rate is 4.63 percent.

Corporate Taxes

Tax Forms: http://www.revenue.state.co.us/forms_download.html

Colorado recognizes the federal S corporation provision. The Subchapter S election is automatic and no state-specific forms need be filed to make the Subchapter S election.

S Corporations

Connecticut

Connecticut Secretary of State
30 Trinity Street
Hartford CT 06106
(860) 509-6002
http://www.sots.state.ct.us/

Incorporating Fee

The fee for filing articles of incorporation (called a certificate of incorporation in Connecticut) is $275. The certificate of incorporation form carries a $200 filing fee, which includes a $150.00 minimum franchise tax and $50 to file the certificate of incorporation. Connecticut imposes an additional filing requirement: an Organization and First Report, which carries an additional filling fee of $75.

Name Reservation

The Connecticut Secretary of State's office provides informal information regarding corporate name availability by calling (860) 509-6002. Connecticut incorporators may reserve corporate names by filing the form entitled, Application for Reservation of Name for Domestic or Foreign Stock & Non-Stock Corp., The fee is $30, and the name reservation remains effective for 120 days.

Corporate Forms: http://www.sots.state.ct.us/Forms/forms.html

Periodic Reporting Requirements

Connecticut corporations and qualified foreign corporations must file annual reports by the last day of the month in which the entity originally filed in the state. The annual report fee is $75. Annual report forms are not available online.

Corporate Taxes

Connecticut corporations and foreign corporations doing business in Connecticut pay a tax based either upon net income or upon capital stock, whichever is higher. The minimum tax is $250.

Tax Forms: http://www.drs.state.ct.us/pubs/formsonline/aspmailrequest.htm

S Corporations

Connecticut recently phased out business tax on S corporations. Connecticut recognizes the federal S corporation provision. The Subchapter S election is automatic and no state-specific forms need be filed to make the Subchapter S election.

District of Columbia

Corporations Division
District of Columbia
Department of Consumer Regulatory Affairs
941 North Capitol Street, N.E.
Washington, DC 20002
(202) 442-4430
http://www.dcra.org/main.shtm

Incorporating Fee

The fee for filing articles of incorporation is $100, plus a minimum license fee of $20, which varies with the amount of authorized stock. The $20 license fee covers up to $100,000 of authorized stock. The Department of Consumer Regulatory Affairs offers a helpful "Articles of Incorporation Instruction Sheet" on their website.

Name Reservation

District of Columbia incorporators may pay a $25 fee to reserve a corporate name by filing an Application for Reservation of Corporate Name. The form is available on the Department of Consumer Regulatory Affairs' website. The name reservation remains effective for 60 days.

Corporate Forms: http://www.dcra.org/bracorp.shtm

Periodic Reporting Requirements

District of Columbia corporations and qualified foreign corporations must file an Annual Report for Foreign and Domestic Corporations with the Department of Consumer Regulatory Affairs. Corporate reports are due by April 15. The filing fee is $100.

Corporate Taxes

District of Columbia corporations and foreign corporations doing business in the District of Columbia are required to file Form D-20, Corporation Franchise Tax Return, by the 15th day of the third month following the close of the taxable year. Annual corporate taxes are based on income, not on shares of stock. The tax rate is 9.975 percent of income attributable to DC operations, and the minimum tax is $100.

Tax Forms: http://cfo.washingtondc.gov/services/tax/forms/frames/forms2.shtm

S Corporations

The District of Columbia recognizes the federal S corporation provision. The Subchapter S election is automatic and no state-specific forms need to be filed to make the Subchapter S election.

Delaware

Division of Corporations
Corporate Filing Section
Delaware Secretary of State
John G. Townsend Building
P.O. Box 898
Dover, DE 19903
(302) 739-3073
http://www.state.de.us/sos/corp.htm

Incorporating Fee

The fee for filing articles of incorporation is $74; this includes the state tax and filing fee of $50, county recording fees of $15, and a $9 document fee. Delaware offers a range of expedited options. See their website for more information.

Name Reservation

Delaware incorporators may pay a $10 name reservation fee by calling (900) 420-8042. You may reserve up to three names. The name reservation remains effective for 30 days.

Corporate Forms: http://www.state.de.us/corp/incbook.htm

Periodic Reporting Requirements

A domestic corporation's annual report is due in March. Forms are mailed to resident agents in January.

Corporate Taxes

All corporations incorporated in the state of Delaware are required to file an Annual Franchise Tax Report and to pay a franchise tax. Taxes and annual reports are to be received no later than March 1 each year. The minimum tax is $30 with a maximum of $150,000. Taxes are based on the number of shares of stock issued. Corporations with 3,000 authorized shares or less automatically pay the minimum of $30. Corporations with more than 3,000 authorized shares pay tax according to an annoyingly complex formula that you may find described at http://www.state.de.us/corp/sch-tax.htm.

Delaware also imposes an income tax, but corporations not conducting business within Delaware are exempt. The Delaware state corporate income tax rate is 8.7 percent of federal taxable income attributable to Delaware activities.

Tax Forms: http://www.state.de.us/revenue/taxformmain.htm

S Corporations

Delaware recognizes the federal S corporation provision. The Subchapter S election is automatic and no state-specific forms need to be filed to make the Subchapter S election. S corporations conducting business in Delaware must file Form 1100S, S Corporation Reconciliation and Shareholders Information Return.

Florida

Division of Corporations
Florida Department of State
409 East Gaines Street
Tallahassee, FL 32399
(850) 488-9000
http://www.dos.state.fl.us/

The fee for filing articles of incorporation is $70. A certified copy fee of $8.75 is optional.

Incorporating Fee

Florida no longer maintains a name reservation program. However, the Secretary of State's website allows free searches of existing corporate names.

Name Reservation

Corporate Forms: http://www.dos.state.fl.us/doc/corp_form.html

Florida recently adopted a new Uniform Business Report, which is due annually. Florida corporations and qualified foreign corporations must file the report by May 1.

Periodic Reporting Requirements

Florida has no franchise tax.

Corporate Taxes

Corporations that conduct business, earn or receive income in Florida, including out-of-state corporations, must file a Florida corporate income tax return. Florida corporate income tax liability is computed using federal taxable income, modified by certain Florida adjustments, to determine adjusted federal income. A corporation doing business within and without Florida may apportion its total income. Adjusted federal income is apportioned to Florida using a three-factor formula. The formula is a weighted average, designating 25 percent each to factors for property and payroll, and 50 percent to sales. Nonbusiness income allocated to Florida is added to the Florida portion of adjusted federal income. An exemption of up to $5,000 is subtracted to arrive at Florida net income. Tax is computed by multiplying Florida net income by 5.5 percent.

Tax Forms: http://sun6.dms.state.fl.us/dor/forms/

Florida recognizes the federal S corporation provision. The Subchapter S election is automatic and no state-specific forms need to be filed to make the Subchapter S election.

S Corporations

Georgia

Corporations Division
Georgia Secretary of State
315 West Tower
2 Martin Luther King, Jr. Drive
Atlanta, GA 30334
(404) 656-2817
(404) 657-2248 (fax)
http://www.sos.state.ga.us/

Incorporating Fee

The fee for filing articles of incorporation is $60.

Name Reservation

All corporations must publish a notice of intent to incorporate in the newspaper which is the official legal organ of the county where the initial registered office of the corporation is to be located, or in a newspaper of general circulation in such county and for which at least 60 percent of its subscriptions are paid. The Clerk of Superior Court can advise you as to the legal organ in your county. The notice of intent to incorporate and a $40 publication fee should be forwarded directly to the newspaper no later than the next business day after filing articles of incorporation with the secretary of state.

Georgia incorporators may informally search existing corporate names on the Georgia Secretary of State's website. Georgia does not charge for reserving corporate names. Georgia incorporators may reserve names online for free by visiting:

http://www.sos.state.ga.us/cgi-bin/namerequest.asp

The name reservation remains effective for 90 days.

Corporate Forms: http://www.sos.state.ga.us/corporations/forms.htm

See http://www.sos.state.ga.us/corporations/corpfil1.htm for sample Georgia articles of incorporation.

Periodic Reporting Requirements

Annual reports are due by April 1 of each year. Corporations must also make an original report within 90 days of incorporation. The annual registration fee is $15. Online filing is available through the Georgia Secretary of State's website.

Corporate Taxes

Georgia corporate taxes have two components. The first is a 6 percent income tax, and the second is a graduated tax based on corporate net worth.

Tax Forms: http://www2.state.ga.us/departments/dor/forms.shtml

S Corporations

Georgia recognizes the federal S corporation provision. The Subchapter S election is automatic and no state-specific forms need to be filed to make the Subchapter S election. S corporations must file a special tax return on Form 600-S.

Hawaii

Business Registration Division
Department of Commerce and Consumer Affairs
1010 Richards Street
Honolulu, Hawaii 96813
(808) 586-2744
(808) 586-2733 (fax)
http://www.hawaii.gov/dcca/

The fee for filing articles of incorporation is $100.

Incorporating Fee

Hawaii incorporators may reserve a corporate name by filing Form X-1 with the Business Registration Division along with a $20 filing fee. The name reservation remains effective for 120 days.

Name Reservation

Corporate Forms: http://www.businessregistrations.com/Registering/registering.html

Hawaii corporations and qualified foreign corporations must file an annual report by March 31 with the Business Registration Division. The filing fee is $25.

Periodic Reporting Requirements

Hawaii corporations and foreign corporations doing business in Hawaii are subject to a corporate income tax. The corporate tax rate is 4.4 percent of income up to $25,000, 5.4 percent of taxable income up to $100,000, 6.4 percent of income exceeding $100,000.

Corporate Taxes

Tax Forms: http://www.state.hi.us/tax/taxforms.html

Hawaii recognizes the federal S corporation provision. The Subchapter S election is automatic and no state-specific forms need to be filed to make the Subchapter S election.

S Corporations

Idaho

Office of the Secretary of State
700 W Jefferson, Room 203
P.O. Box 83720
Boise, ID 83720-0080
(208) 334-2300
(208) 334-2282 (fax)
http://www.idsos.state.id.us/

Incorporating Fee

The fee for filing articles of incorporation is $100.

Name Reservation

Idaho incorporators may reserve a corporate name by filing an Application for Reservation of Legal Entity Name and paying a $20 fee. The name reservation remains effective for four months.

Corporate Forms: http://www.idsos.state.id.us/corp/corindex.htm

Periodic Reporting Requirements

Idaho corporations and qualified foreign corporations must file an annual corporate report. The report is due in the anniversary month of incorporation or qualification. If timely, the report has no filing fee. The secretary of state's office mails the form two months before its due date.

Corporate Taxes

Idaho corporations and foreign corporations doing business in Idaho must pay a corporate income tax. The income tax rate is 8 percent.

Tax Forms: http://www2.state.id.us/tax/forms.htm

S Corporations

Idaho recognizes the federal S corporation provision. The Subchapter S election is automatic and no state-specific forms need to be filed to make the Subchapter S election.

Illinois

Department of Business Services
Illinois Secretary of State
501 S. Second St., Suite 328
Springfield, IL 62756
(217) 782-6961
http://www.sos.state.il.us/services/services_business.html

The fee for filing articles of incorporation is $75, plus franchise tax. The initial franchise tax is assessed at the rate of 15/100 of 1 percent ($150 per $1,000) on the paid-in capital represented in Illinois, with a minimum of $25. The Department of Business Services in Springfield will provide assistance in calculating the total fee, if necessary. Call (217) 782-9522 or 9523 for assistance.

Incorporating Fee

Illinois incorporators may reserve a corporate name by filing Form BCA-4.10 with the Illinois Secretary of State and paying a $25 fee per reserved name. The name reservation remains effective for 90 days.

Name Reservation

Corporate Forms: http://www.sos.state.il.us/depts/bus_serv/forms.html

Domestic corporations must file a Domestic Corporation Annual Report annually, and qualified foreign corporations must file a Foreign Corporation Annual Report annually.

Periodic Reporting Requirements

Illinois corporations and foreign corporations doing business in Illinois must pay an income tax and a "replacement" tax based upon the value of the corporation's gross assets in Illinois and the gross amount of business transacted in the state.

Corporate Taxes

Franchise tax is reported on the annual report form, discussed above.

Tax Forms: http://www.revenue.state.il.us/

Illinois recognizes the federal S corporation provision. The Subchapter S election is automatic and no state-specific forms need be filed to make the Subchapter S election.

S Corporations

Indiana

Corporations Division
Indiana Secretary of State
302 West Washington Street, Room E018
Indianapolis, IN 46204
(317) 232-6576
http://www.state.in.us/sos/

Incorporating Fee

The fee for filing articles of incorporation is $90.

Name Reservation

Indiana offers free preliminary name availability information by telephone at (317) 232-6576. Indiana incorporators may reserve a corporate name by filing a name reservation application along with a $20 fee. The reservation is effective for 120 days.

Corporate Forms: http://www.state.in.us/sos/forms/forms.html

Periodic Reporting Requirements

Indiana corporations and qualified foreign corporations must file a biennial corporate report with the Indiana Secretary of State along with a $30 fee.

Corporate Taxes

Indiana corporations and foreign corporations doing business in Indiana must pay two corporate income taxes: a corporate income tax based upon gross income, and an adjusted gross income tax. The gross income tax has two rates, a high rate of 1.2 percent and a low rate of .3 percent. The adjusted gross income tax rate is 3.4 percent.

Tax Forms: http://www.state.in.us/dor/forms/forms.html

S Corporations

Indiana recognizes the S corporation provision. Indiana corporations must elect to be deemed "special" corporation (equivalent to an S corporation) using Form IT-20SC. Indiana special corporations are exempt from the gross income tax.

Iowa

Business Services Division
Office of the Secretary of State
1305 E Walnut
Hoover Building, 2nd Floor
Des Moines, IA 50319
(515) 281-5204
http://www.sos.state.ia.us/

The fee for filing articles of incorporation is $50.	**Incorporating Fee**
Iowa incorporators may reserve a name by filing an Application to Reserve Corporate Name and paying a $10 fee. The name reservation remains effective for 120 days. Corporate Forms: http://www.sos.state.ia.us/business/corpform.html	**Name Reservation**
Iowa corporations and qualified foreign corporations must file a biennial corporate report with the secretary of state. Reports are due between January and April 1 of even-numbered years following the year of incorporation. The report filing fee is $45.	**Periodic Reporting Requirements**
Iowa corporations and foreign corporations doing business in Iowa must pay a corporate income tax. The corporate income tax rate ranges from 6 to 12 percent. For more information, contact the Iowa Department of Revenue at (515) 281-3114, or visit the department's website. Tax Forms: http://www.state.ia.us/government/drf/index.html	**Corporate Taxes**
Iowa recognizes the federal S corporation provision. The Subchapter S election is automatic and no state-specific forms need be filed to make the Subchapter S election.	**S Corporations**
Iowa's Department of Revenue & Finance publishes an informative guide to starting a business in Iowa at http://www.state.ia.us/government/drf/business/newbus.html	**Additional Information**

Kansas

Corporation Division
Kansas Secretary of State
Memorial Hall, First Floor
120 S. W. 10th Ave.
Topeka, KS 66612-1594
(785) 296-4564
(785) 296-4570 (fax)
http://www.kssos.org/

Incorporating Fee

The fee for filing articles of incorporation is $75.

Name Reservation

Kansas incorporators may reserve a corporate name by filing Form NR with the Kansas Secretary of State and paying a $20 fee. The name reservation remains effective for 120 days.

Corporate Forms: http://www.kssos.org/corpdown.html

Periodic Reporting Requirements

Kansas corporations must file a recently simplified Form AR, Corporate Annual Report, and must pay a minimum franchise tax of $20.

Corporate Taxes

Kansas corporations and foreign corporations doing business in Kansas must pay a franchise tax based upon the net worth of the company. The minimum franchise tax is $20, and the maximum is $2,500. Kansas corporations are also subject to a corporate income tax, payable annually on Form K120.

Tax Forms: http://www.kssos.org/corpdown.html and
http://www.ink.org/public/kdor/taxforms.html

S Corporations

Kansas recognizes the federal S corporation provision. The Subchapter S election is automatic and no state-specific forms need be filed to make the Subchapter S election. Corporations that elect Subchapter S status must file Form K120S, Kansas Small Business Income Tax Return.

Additional Information

Kansas publishes a thorough and helpful *Kansas Corporate Handbook,* available from the secretary of state's website.

Kentucky

Kentucky Secretary of State
700 Capital Avenue
Suite 152, State Capitol
Frankfort, KY 40601
(502) 564-3490
(502) 564-5687 (fax)
http://www.sos.state.ky.us/

Incorporating Fee

The fee for filing articles of incorporation is $40, plus an organization tax based on number of authorized shares. The organization tax is as follows: $.01 per share up to 20,000 shares, $.005 per share on the next 180,000 shares, $.002 per share on the remaining shares, with a minimum tax fee of $10 for 1,000 shares or less.

Name Reservation

Kentucky incorporators may reserve a corporate name by filing Form SSC-105, Application for Reserved Name, with the Kentucky Secretary of State along with a $15 fee. The name reservation remains effective for 120 days. Informal searches are available online and by calling (502) 564-2848.

Corporate Forms: http://www.sos.state.ky.us/BUSSER/BUSFIL/FORMS.HTM

Periodic Reporting Requirements

Kentucky corporations and qualified foreign corporations must file an annual report, due by June 30 of each year beginning with the calendar year following the date of the corporation's formation or qualification. The filing fee is $15. The annual report form is not available online, the secretary of state's office mails the form to registered agents between January and March of each year.

Corporate Taxes

Kentucky corporations and foreign corporations doing business in Kentucky are subject to an income tax, payable annually on Form 720. The tax rate is progressive, beginning at 4 percent and graduating to 8.25 percent.

Tax Forms: http://www.state.ky.us/agencies/revenue/taxforms.htm

S Corporations

Kentucky recognizes the federal S corporation provision. The Subchapter S election is automatic and no state-specific forms need be filed to make the Subchapter S election.

Louisiana

Commercial Division
Louisiana Secretary of State
P.O. Box 94125
Baton Rouge, LA 70804
(225) 925-4704
http://www.sec.state.la.us/

Incorporating Fee

The fee for filing articles of incorporation is $60. Corporations must also file Form 341, Domestic Corporation Initial Report, concurrently with the articles. If a corporation does not name directors in its Domestic Corporation Initial Report, then the corporation must disclose its directors in a Corporation Supplemental Initial Report.

Name Reservation

Informal inquiries regarding corporate name availability may be made by phone (225) 925-4704, by fax (225) 925-4727, or by mail to P.O. Box 94125, Baton Rouge, LA 70804. Louisiana incorporators may reserve a corporate name by filing Form 398. Reservations are effective for 60 days. Two 30-day extensions are available upon request. The fee for reservations is $20 each.

Corporate Forms: http://www.sec.state.la.us/comm/corp-index.htm

Periodic Reporting Requirements

Louisiana corporations and qualified foreign corporations must file annual reports before the anniversary date of incorporation or qualification in Louisiana. The secretary of state mails the form to the corporation at least 60 days prior to the anniversary date. The secretary of state does not provide blank forms. The filing fee is $25.

Corporate Taxes

Louisiana corporations and foreign corporations doing business in Louisiana are subject to corporate franchise tax and corporate income tax. The franchise tax is calculated as follows: $1.50 for each $1,000 of capital employed in Louisiana up to $300,000, and $3.00 for each $1,000 of capital employed in Louisiana in excess of $300,000. The income tax rate is progressive, beginning at 4 percent and graduating to 8 percent.

Tax Forms: http://www.rev.state.la.us/TaxForm.htm

S Corporations

Louisiana recognizes the federal S corporation provision. No state-specific forms are required to effect the Subchapter S election. Louisiana taxes S corporations in the same manner as regular corporations, with one exception. A corporation classified by the IRS as an S corporation may be entitled to an exclusion of part or all of its income for Louisiana income tax purposes, depending on the percentage of shares owned by Louisiana resident individuals. In general terms, the portion of income that can be excluded is determined by the ratio of outstanding shares owned by Louisiana resident individuals to total shares outstanding.

Maine

Bureau of Corporations
Maine State Department
101 State House Station
Augusta, ME 04333
(207) 287-3676
(207) 287-5874 (fax)
http://www.state.me.us/sos/

Incorporating Fee

The fee for filing articles of incorporation is $95, plus a minimum fee of $30 based upon authorized shares of stock.

Name Reservation

Maine incorporators may reserve a corporate name by filing Form MBCA1 with the Bureau of Corporations along with a $20 fee. The name reservation remains effective for 120 days.

Corporate Forms: http://www.state.me.us/sos/cec/corp/formfees.htm

Periodic Reporting Requirements

Maine corporations must file an annual report on Form MBCA 13. The filing fee is $60. The form is not available online. The Maine State Department mails annual reports to corporations each year.

Corporate Taxes

Maine corporations and foreign corporations doing business in Maine are subject to an income tax.

Tax Forms: http://janus.state.me.us/revenue/forms/homepage.html

S Corporations

Maine recognizes the federal S corporation provision. The Subchapter S election is automatic and no state-specific forms need be filed to make the Subchapter S election. Maine S corporations must file an information return on Form 1120S-ME.

Maryland

Maryland Secretary of State
301 West Preston Street
Baltimore, MD 21201
(410) 974-5521
(888) 874-0013
(410) 974-5190 (fax)
http://www.sos.state.md.us/

Incorporating Fee

The fee to file articles of incorporation is $40 unless the aggregate par value of the stock exceeds $100,000 or, if no par value stock is used, the corporation has authority to issue more than 5,000 shares. If stock exceeds these amounts, call (410) 767-1340 for the fee.

Name Reservation

Maryland incorporators may reserve a corporate name by paying a $7 fee. The name reservation remains effective for 30 days.

Corporate Forms: http://www.dat.state.md.us/sdatweb/charter.html

Periodic Reporting Requirements

Maryland corporations and qualified foreign corporations must file an annual Form 1, Personal Property Report, no later than April 15. The filing fee is $100.

Corporate Taxes

Maryland corporations and foreign corporations with Maryland income must pay a corporate income tax. The tax rate is 7 percent.

Tax Forms: http://www.comp.state.md.us/forms/default.asp

S Corporations

Maryland recognizes the federal S corporation provision. The Subchapter S election is automatic and no state-specific forms need be filed to make the Subchapter S election.

Massachusetts

Corporations Division
Massachusetts Secretary of State
One Ashburton Place
Boston, MA 02108
(617) 727-9640
http://www.state.ma.us/sec/

The fee for filing articles of incorporation is a minimum of $200.   **Incorporating Fee**

Massachusetts incorporators may reserve a corporate name by paying a   **Name Reservation**
$15 fee.

Corporate Forms: http://www.state.ma.us/sec/cor/cordpc/dpcfrm.htm

Massachusetts corporations must file a Massachusetts Corporation   **Periodic Reporting**
Annual Report, which is due on or before the 15th day of the third   **Requirements**
month after the close of the corporation's fiscal year. The filing fee is
$85. A fillable form is available online at http://www.state.ma.us/sec/
cor/cordpc/dpcfrm.htm.

Massachusetts corporations and foreign corporations with taxable oper-   **Corporate Taxes**
ations in Massachusetts must pay a corporate excise tax. Corporations
incorporated within the commonwealth of Massachusetts file Form
355A. Corporations chartered in foreign states file Form 355B. The
excise tax is calculated as follows: $2.60 per $1,000 of taxable Massachusetts tangible property, and 9.5 percent of income attributable to
Massachusetts.

Tax Forms: http://www.state.ma.us/dor/forms/taxform.htm

Massachusetts recognizes the federal S corporation provision. The Sub-   **S Corporations**
chapter S election is automatic and no state-specific forms need be filed
to make the Subchapter S election.

Michigan

Corporations Division
Bureau of Commercial Services
6546 Mercantile Way
Lansing, MI 48911
Mailing Address:
7150 Harris Drive
P.O. Box 30054
Lansing, MI 48909
(517) 241-6470
(517) 334-8048 (Mich-ELF fax filing service)
http://www.commerce.state.mi.us/bcs/corp/

Incorporating Fee

The fee for filing articles of incorporation is $60, up to 20,000 authorized shares of stock.

Name Reservation

Michigan incorporators may reserve a corporate name by completing and filing Form C&S-540, Application for Reservation of Name, with the Corporations Division accompanied by a $10 fee.

Corporate Forms: http://www.commerce.state.mi.us/bcs/corp/corpindx.htm

Periodic Reporting Requirements

Michigan corporations must file a simplified annual report form. The annual report form is not available online. The Michigan Bureau of Commercial Services mails the form to corporations each year. The form carries a $15 charge.

Corporate Taxes

Corporations engaged in a business activity in Michigan whose adjusted gross receipts are $250,000 or more in a tax year are required to file a Single Business Tax (SBT) return.

Tax Forms: http://www.treas.state.mi.us/formspub/formind.htm

S Corporations

Michigan recognizes the federal S corporation provision. The Subchapter S election is automatic and no state-specific forms need be filed to make the Subchapter S election. However, S corporations remain subject to the SBT.

Additional Information

Michigan operates an Electronic Filing System by facsimile (Mich-ELF). For more information, see http://www.commerce.state.mi.us/bcs/corp/elf-faq.htm

Minnesota

Minnesota Secretary of State
180 State Office Building
St. Paul, MN 55155-1299
(651) 296-2803
(877) 551-6767
http://www.sos.state.mn.us/

The fee for filing articles of incorporation is $135.   **Incorporating Fee**

Minnesota incorporators may reserve a corporate name by filing a   **Name Reservation**
Request for Reservation of Name with the Minnesota Secretary of State
and paying a $35 filing fee. The name reservation remains effective for
one year.

Corporate Forms: http://www.sos.state.mn.us/business/forms.html

Minnesota corporations must file a Domestic Corporation Annual Reg-   **Periodic Reporting**
istration by December 31 of each year. There is no filing fee. Foreign cor-   **Requirements**
porations must file a Foreign Corporation Annual Registration by De-
cember 31 of each year. The filing fee is $115.

Minnesota corporations are subject to an annual corporate franchise tax.   **Corporate Taxes**

Tax Forms: http://www.taxes.state.mn.us/99forms.html

Minnesota recognizes the federal S corporation provision. The Subchap-   **S Corporations**
ter S election is automatic and no state-specific forms need be filed to
make the Subchapter S election.

Mississippi

Mississippi Secretary of State
P.O. Box 136
Jackson, MS 39205
(601) 359-1350
(601) 359-1499 (fax)
http://www.sos.state.ms.us/

Incorporating Fee   The fee for filing articles of incorporation is $50.

Name Reservation   Mississippi incorporators may reserve a corporation name by filing Form F0016, Reservation of Name with the Mississippi Secretary of State. The filing fee is $25. The name reservation remains effective for 180 days.

                              Corporate Forms: http://www.sos.state.ms.us/forms/omni_instruct.html

**Periodic Reporting
Requirements**   Mississippi corporations and qualified foreign corporations must file a Corporate Annual Report, which is due April 1. The filing fee is $25.

Corporate Taxes   Mississippi corporations and foreign corporations doing business in Mississippi must pay an income tax and a franchise tax. The minimum franchise tax is $25.

                              Tax Forms: http://www.mstc.state.ms.us/downloadforms/main.htm

S Corporations   Mississippi does not recognize the federal S corporation provision.

Missouri

Missouri Corporations Division
P.O. Box 778
Jefferson City, MO 65102
(573) 751-4153
http://mosl.sos.state.mo.us/bus-ser/soscor.html

The minimum fee for filing articles of incorporation is $58.

Incorporating Fee

Missouri incorporators may reserve a corporate name by filing an Application for Reservation of Name with the Missouri Corporations Division. The filing fee is $25. The name reservation remains effective for 60 days.

Name Reservation

Corporate Forms: http://mosl.sos.state.mo.us/sosforms.html

Missouri corporations and qualified foreign corporations must file an annual registration report. Annual reports are due by the 15th day of the fourth month of the corporation's fiscal year. The secretary of state's office mails the form to the corporation's registered agent. The form is not available online.

Periodic Reporting Requirements

Missouri corporations and foreign corporations doing business in Missouri pay both a franchise and income tax.

Corporate Taxes

Tax Forms: http://dor.state.mo.us/tax/redesign.htm

Missouri recognizes the federal S corporation provision. The Subchapter S election is automatic and no state-specific forms need be filed to make the Subchapter S election. Missouri S corporations must file Form MO-1120S.

S Corporations

Montana

Business Services Bureau
P.O. Box 202801
Helena, Montana 59620-2801
(406) 444-2034
(406) 444-3976
http://www.state.mt.us/sos/

Incorporating Fee

The minimum fee for filing articles of incorporation is $70, which includes a filing fee of $20 and a license fee of $50 for up to 50,000 authorized shares.

Name Reservation

Montana incorporators may reserve a corporate name by filing an Application for Reservation of Name with the Business Services Bureau accompanied by a $10 filing fee. The name reservation remains effective for 120 days.

Corporate Forms: http://www.state.mt.us/sos/Business_Services/forms.html

Periodic Reporting Requirements

Montana corporations and qualified foreign corporations must file an Annual Corporation Report accompanied by a $10 fee.

Corporate Taxes

Montana corporations and foreign corporations doing business in Montana must pay a corporation license tax, which is based upon corporate income attributable to Montana.

Tax Forms: http://www.state.mt.us/revenue/forms_downloadable.htm

S Corporations

Montana recognizes the federal S corporation provision. The Subchapter S election is automatic and no state-specific forms need be filed to make the Subchapter S election.

Nebraska

Nebraska Corporate Division
Nebraska Secretary of State
State Capitol, Room 1305
P.O. Box 94608
Lincoln, NE 68509-4608
(402) 471-4079
(402) 471-3666 (fax)
http://www.nol.org/home/SOS/

The minimum fee for filing articles of incorporation is $60, which includes up to $10,000 in authorized capital. Authorized capital is the total authorized shares multiplied by the share's par value.

Incorporating Fee

Nebraska incorporators may reserve a corporate name by filing an Application for Reservation of Corporate Name with the Nebraska Corporate Division accompanied by a filing fee of $30. The name reservation remains effective for 120 days.

Name Reservation

Corporate Forms: http://www.nol.org/home/SOS/corps/corpform.htm

Nebraska corporations and qualified foreign corporations must file an annual corporation occupation tax report. The fee is based upon the paid up capital stock (for domestic corporations) and the real estate and personal property in use in Nebraska (for foreign corporations).

Periodic Reporting Requirements

Nebraska corporations and foreign corporations doing business in Nebraska are subject to an income tax.

Corporate Taxes

Tax Forms: http://www.nol.org/home/NDR/tax/forms.htm

Nebraska recognizes the federal S corporation provision. The Subchapter S election is automatic and no state-specific forms need be filed to make the Subchapter S election.

S Corporations

Nevada

Nevada Secretary of State
101 North Carson Street, Suite 3
Carson City, NV 89701-4786
(775) 684-5708
http://sos.state.nv.us/

Incorporating Fee

The fee for filing articles of incorporation is $175, but graduates upward based on the authorized capital. Authorized capital is the total authorized shares multiplied by the shares' par value. Nevada corporations must file an Initial List of Officers, Directors and Resident Agent. Corporations must file the form by the first day of the second month following the incorporation date. The filing fee is $165.

Name Reservation

Nevada incorporators may reserve a corporate name by paying a $20 fee. The name reservation can be effected through the secretary of state's website. The name reservation remains effective for 90 days.

Corporate Forms: http://sos.state.nv.us/comm_rec/crforms/crforms.htm

Periodic Reporting Requirements

Nevada corporations must file an Annual List of Officers form, which is due by the end of the anniversary month of the corporation's initial filing. The filing fee is $85.

Corporate Taxes

Nevada has one of the least burdensome tax structures in the United States. Nevada has no corporate income tax, and no corporate franchise tax.

S Corporations

Because Nevada does not impose a corporate income tax, S corporation status is not relevant to Nevada taxation.

New Hampshire

State Corporation Division
New Hampshire Secretary of State
Statehouse, Room 204
Concord, NH 03301
(603) 271-3244
http://webster.state.nh.us/sos/

The fee for filing articles of incorporation is $85. Note that articles of incorporation must accompany Form 11-A, Addendum to Articles of Incorporation. Form 11-A requires the incorporator(s) to vouch for the corporation's registration or exemption from the state's securities laws.

Incorporating Fee

The Corporation Division provides informal information on corporate name availability at (603) 271-3246. New Hampshire incorporators may reserve a corporate name by filing Form 1, Application for Reservation of Name, accompanied by a $15 filing fee. The name reservation remains effective for 120 days.

Name Reservation

Corporate Forms: http://www.state.nh.us/sos/corporate/index.htm

New Hampshire corporations and qualified foreign corporations must file an annual report form. The form is not available online. The State Corporation Division mails the form in January of each year. The form is due April 1 of each year. The filing fee is $100.

Periodic Reporting Requirements

New Hampshire corporations and foreign corporations doing business in New Hampshire must pay an income tax called a business profits tax. The tax rate is 8 percent. However, organizations with $50,000 or less of gross receipts from all their activities in New Hampshire are not required to file a return. In addition, corporations are subject to a business enterprise tax. The business enterprise tax is a 0.50 percent tax assessed on the enterprise value tax base, which is the sum of all compensation paid or accrued, interest paid or accrued, and dividends paid by the business enterprise, after special adjustments and apportionment.

Corporate Taxes

Tax Forms: http://webster.state.nh.us/revenue/forms/forms.htm

New Hampshire does not recognize the federal S corporation provision.

S Corporations

New Jersey

New Jersey Division of Revenue
Business Services
225 West State Street
Trenton, NJ 08608-1001
(609) 292-9292
(609) 984-6851 (fax)
http://www.state.nj.us/treasury/revenue/dcr/dcrpg1.html

Incorporating Fee

The fee for filing articles of incorporation is $100.

Name Reservation

New Jersey incorporators may reserve a corporate name by filling out a Business Entity Name Availability Check & Reservation at the Business Services website at http://www.state.nj.us/njbgs/njbgsnar.htm. The fee is $50. The name reservation remains effective for 120 days.

New Jersey does not offer corporate forms online. Customers may order forms over the telephone by calling (609) 292-9292 and following the prompts. Annual report forms may only be obtained by writing to P.O. Box 302, Trenton, NJ 08625 or by faxing your request to (609) 984-6849. Remember to include the following information in your request: return address; name of the business; and the ten-digit identification number, if known.

Periodic Reporting Requirements

New Jersey corporations and qualified foreign corporations must file an annual report accompanied by a $40 fee.

Corporate Taxes

New Jersey corporations and foreign corporations doing business in New Jersey must pay a corporate business tax (CBT). The CBT rate is 9 percent on the adjusted net income attributable to new Jersey operations.

Tax Forms: http://www.state.nj.us/treasury/taxation/forms.htm

S Corporations

New Jersey requires state-specific forms to recognize the federal S corporation provision, specifically, Form CBT- 2553, New Jersey S Corporation Election. Further information on New Jersey S corporations is available at:

http://www.state.nj.us/treasury/taxation/ot5.htm

New Mexico

Corporations Division
1120 Paseo De Peralta
P.O. Box 1269
Santa Fe, New Mexico 87504
(505) 827-4508
(800) 947-4722
http://www.nmprc.state.nm.us/

The minimum fee for filing articles of incorporation is one dollar for each 1,000 authorized shares of stock, with a minimum filing fee $100, and a maximum filing fee of $1,000.

Incorporating Fee

New Mexico incorporators may reserve a corporate name by filing a Reservation of Corporate Name form with the Corporations Division. The form is not available online, but is available by calling (505) 827-4504 or 4509. The filing fee is $25. The name reservation remains effective for 120 days.

Name Reservation

Corporate Forms: http://www.nmprc.state.nm.us/forms.htm

New Mexico corporations and qualified foreign corporations must file a First Report within 30 days from the date of incorporation or qualification in New Mexico. The filing fee is $25. Thereafter, New Mexico corporations and qualified foreign corporations must file a biennial report on or before the 15th day of the third month following the end of the corporation's fiscal year.

Periodic Reporting Requirements

New Mexico corporations and foreign corporations doing business in New Mexico are subject to a corporate franchise tax and a corporate income tax. The corporate franchise tax is $50 per year. The income tax rate is progressive and ranges from 4.8 percent of net income to 7.6 percent of net income.

Corporate Taxes

Tax Forms: http://www.state.nm.us/tax/trd_form.htm

New Mexico recognizes the federal S corporation provision. The Subchapter S election is automatic and no state-specific forms need be filed to make the Subchapter S election. S corporations remain subject to the corporate franchise tax.

S Corporations

New York

Division of Corporations
New York Department of State
41 State Street
Albany, NY 12231-0001
(518) 474-2492
(518) 474-1418
http://www.dos.state.ny.us/

Incorporating Fee

The fee for filing a certificate of incorporation is $125, plus the applicable tax on shares pursuant to Section 180 of New York's tax law. Contact the Division of Corporations for more information.

Name Reservation

New York incorporators may reserve a corporate name by filing an Application for Reservation of Name form with the Division of Corporations accompanied by a filing fee of $20. The name reservation remains effective for 60 days.

Corporate Forms: http://www.dos.state.ny.us/

Periodic Reporting Requirements

New York corporations and qualified foreign corporations must file a biennial statement accompanied by a $9 filing fee. The statement is due in the calendar month in which the corporation filed its original certificate of incorporation.

Corporate Taxes

New York corporations and foreign corporations doing business in New York must pay an annual maintenance fee tax, a corporate franchise tax, and an income tax. Foreign corporations are also subject to a New York State license fee, and domestic corporations are also subject to an organization tax. New York taxation is onerous and complex, so contact the New York Department of Taxation and Finance for more information.

Tax Forms: http://www.tax.state.ny.us/Forms/corp_cur_forms.htm

S Corporations

New York requires corporations to file Form CT-6, Election by a Federal S Corporation, to be treated as a New York S Corporation, to elect S corporation status.

North Carolina

Corporations Division
North Carolina Secretary of State
P.O. Box 29622
Raleigh, NC 27626-0622
(919) 807-2225
(888) 246 7636 (call back line)
http://www.secstate.state.nc.us/

The fee for filing articles of incorporation is $125.

Incorporating Fee

North Carolina incorporators may reserve a corporate name by filing an Application to Reserve a Corporate Name accompanied by a filing fee of $10. The name reservation remains effective for 120 days.

Name Reservation

Corporate Forms: http://www.secretary.state.nc.us/corporations/indxfees.asp

North Carolina corporations and qualified foreign corporations must file an annual report with the secretary of state.

Periodic Reporting Requirements

North Carolina corporations and foreign corporations doing business in North Carolina must pay a franchise tax and an income tax. The franchise tax rate is $1.50 of each $1,000 of the capital stock, surplus, and undivided profits base—essentially a tax on corporate property. The minimum franchise tax is $35. The income tax rate is 6.9 percent.

Corporate Taxes

Tax Forms: http://www.dor.state.nc.us/forms/

North Carolina recognizes the federal S corporation provision. The Subchapter S election is automatic and no state-specific forms need be filed to make the Subchapter S election.

S Corporations

North Dakota

North Dakota Secretary of State
600 East Boulevard
Bismarck, ND 58505-0500
(701) 328-4284
(800) 352-0867, ext. 8-3365
(701) 328-2992 (fax)
http://www.state.nd.us/sec/

Incorporating Fee

The minimum fee for filing articles of incorporation is $90. This includes a $30 filing fee, a $10 consent of agent fee, and a $50 minimum license fee. The license fee is based upon the number of authorized shares. Incorporators must include with their filing a Registered Agent Consent to Serve form.

Name Reservation

North Dakota incorporators may reserve a corporate name by filing Form SFN13015, Reserve Name Application with the North Dakota Secretary of State accompanied by a filing fee of $10. The name reservation remains effective for twelve months.

Corporate Forms: http://www.state.nd.us/sec/Business/forms/businessinforegformsmnu.htm

Periodic Reporting Requirements

North Dakota corporations and qualified foreign corporations must file an annual report each year following the year in which they were incorporated or qualified. Annual report forms are not available on the secretary of state's website. The report is due on August 1. The filing fee is $25.

Corporate Taxes

North Dakota corporations and foreign corporations doing business in North Dakota must pay an annual corporate income tax, and a license fee based upon the corporation's authorized shares.

Tax Forms: http://www.state.nd.us/taxdpt/forms/forms.htm

S Corporations

North Dakota recognizes the federal S corporation provision. The Subchapter S election is automatic and no state specific forms need be filed to make the Subchapter S election.

Ohio

Business Services Division
Ohio Secretary of State
180 E. Broad St., 16th Floor
Columbus, OH 43215
(614) 466-3910
(877) 767-3453
(614) 466-3899 (fax)
http://www.state.oh.us/sos/

The fee for filing articles of incorporation is $85 for corporations autho- **Incorporating Fee**
rizing up to 850 shares. For corporations authorizing more than 850
shares, the following fee table applies: For 851 to 1,000 authorized shares,
the filing fee is 10 cents per share. From 1,001 to 10,000 authorized shares,
the filing fee is 5 cents per share. From 10,001 to 50,000 authorized shares,
the filing fee is 2 cents per share. From 50,001 to 100,000 authorized
shares, the filing fee is 1 cent per share. From 100,001 to 500,000 authorized shares, the filing fee is 1/2 cent per share. For all authorized shares
in excess of 500,000 shares, the filing fee is 1/4 cent per share.

Ohio offers informal name availability information by telephone at (614) **Name Reservation**
466-3910 or (877) 767-3453, and by e-mail at busserv@sos.state.oh.us.
Ohio incorporators may reserve a corporate name by sending a written
request (no form is available) to the secretary of state accompanied by a
$5 fee. The name reservation remains effective for 60 days.

The Ohio Secretary of State offers very few corporate forms on its website. The website advises that "Forms for corporation filings may be
obtained from the office of the Secretary of State, either from this web
page or by calling toll free (877) 767-3453. The Ohio Department of
Development's One Stop Business Permit Center at (800) 248-4040 can
provide forms for partnerships, sole proprietorships, corporations and
other business start-up application."

Ohio corporations and qualified foreign corporations must file an an- **Periodic Reporting**
nual report. The annual report form is not available on the secretary of **Requirements**
state's website. Contact the secretary of state's office to obtain an annual
report form.

Ohio corporations and foreign corporations doing business in Ohio **Corporate Taxes**
must pay an annual corporate franchise tax. The franchise tax is based
upon the corporation's income attributable to Ohio operations and the
net worth of the corporation. The minimum tax is $50.

Tax Forms: http://www.state.oh.us/tax/tabforms.htm

Ohio recognizes the federal S corporation provision. Ohio corporations **S Corporations**
and qualified foreign corporations must file Form FT-1120-S, Notice of S
Corporation Status.

Oklahoma

Business Filing Department
Oklahoma Secretary of State
2300 N. Lincoln Blvd., Room 101
Oklahoma City, OK 73105-4897
(405) 522-4560
(405) 521-3771 (fax)
http://www.sos.state.ok.us/

Incorporating Fee

The minimum fee for filing articles of incorporation is $50. Oklahoma bases its filing fee on the corporation's authorized capital. Authorized capital is the total authorized shares multiplied by the share's par value. The filing fee is $1 per $1,000 of authorized capital.

Name Reservation

Oklahoma incorporators may reserve a corporate name by either submitting an Application for Reservation of Name form to the Oklahoma Secretary of State or by telephone. The filing fee is $10. The name reservation remains effective for 60 days.

Corporate Forms: http://www.sos.state.ok.us/forms/FORMS.HTM

Periodic Reporting Requirements

Foreign corporations must file an annual certificate on or before the anniversary date of its qualification in Oklahoma. The secretary of state mails the forms to the corporation's last known address.

Corporate Taxes

Oklahoma levies an annual franchise tax on all corporations that do business in the state. Corporations are taxed $1.25 for each $1,000 of capital invested or used in Oklahoma. Foreign corporations are additionally assessed $100 per year, payable to the Oklahoma Tax Commission, for the secretary of state acting as their registered agent. The franchise tax return, unless an election is made to file in conjunction with the filing of the Oklahoma income tax, is due July 1. Corporations are also subject to an income tax. The tax rate is 6 percent.

Tax Forms: http://www.oktax.state.ok.us/oktax/formsnpub.html

S Corporations

Oklahoma recognizes the S corporation provision. The Subchapter S election is automatic and no state-specific forms need be filed to make the Subchapter S election.

Oregon

Corporation Division
Oregon Office of the Secretary of State
Public Service Building, Suite 151
255 Capitol Street NE
Salem, OR 97310
(503) 986-2200
http://www.sos.state.or.us/

The fee for filing articles of incorporation is $50.   **Incorporating Fee**

Oregon corporations may pay a $10 fee to reserve a name for 120 days.   **Name Reservation**

Corporate forms are not available on the Oregon Secretary of State's website. Contact the office directly to receive forms.

Oregon corporations and qualified foreign corporations must file an annual report by a corporation's anniversary date. The Corporation Division mails annual report forms to corporations approximately 45 days prior to the due date. Corporations must pay a renewal fee. Oregon corporations pay $30 and foreign corporations pay $220.   **Periodic Reporting Requirements**

Oregon corporations and foreign corporations doing business in Oregon must pay an annual corporate income tax. The income tax rate is 6.6 percent.   **Corporate Taxes**

Tax Forms: http://www.dor.state.or.us/forms.html

Oregon recognizes the S corporation provision. The Subchapter S election is automatic and no state-specific forms need be filed to make the Subchapter S election.   **S Corporations**

Pennsylvania

Corporation Bureau
Department of State
Commonwealth Avenue & North Street
308 North Office Building
Harrisburg, PA 17120
(717) 787-1057
http://www.dos.state.pa.us/

Incorporating Fee

The fee for filing articles of incorporation is $100.

Name Reservation

Pennsylvania incorporators may reserve a corporate name by submitting a written or faxed request to the Corporation Bureau. The fee is $52. The name reservation remains effective for 120 days.

Corporate Forms: http://www.dos.state.pa.us/corps/forms.htm

Periodic Reporting Requirements

Pennsylvania corporations and qualified foreign corporations are not required to file annual reports. However, they are required to notify the Corporation Bureau upon a change in the name or address of the registered agent by filing a Statement of Change of Registered Agent.

Corporate Taxes

Pennsylvania corporations and foreign corporations doing business in Pennsylvania must pay a corporate net income tax and a corporate loans tax. The corporate income tax rate changes from year to year, but is generally burdensome. The corporate loans tax is imposed at the rate of 4 mills on each dollar of the nominal value of all scrip, bonds, certificates, and evidences of indebtedness. In addition, Pennsylvania corporations must pay a capital stock tax. The capital stock tax for domestic firms is imposed on the corporation's capital stock value, as derived by the application of a formula. Foreign corporations must remit foreign franchise tax. The foreign franchise tax is a tax on the privilege of doing business in Pennsylvania, rather than on property, and is imposed on the capital stock value attributable to Pennsylvania.

Tax Forms: http://www.revenue.state.pa.us/forms/corporation/index.htm

S Corporations

Pennsylvania requires that corporations file Form REV-1640 to elect S corporation status. Pennsylvania S corporations must file an annual information return of Form PA-20S.

Rhode Island

Corporation Division
Rhode Island Secretary of State
State House, Room 220
Providence, RI 02903
(401) 222-2357
(401) 222-1356 (fax)
http://www.sec.state.ri.us/

Incorporating Fee

The fee for filing articles of incorporation is $150 for up to 8,000 authorized shares. The fee graduates for additional authorized shares.

Name Reservation

Rhode Island incorporators may reserve a corporate name by filing an Application for Reservation of Entity Name with the Corporation Division accompanied by a $50 filing fee. The name reservation remains effective for 120 days.

Corporate Forms: http://155.212.254.78/corpforms.htm

Periodic Reporting Requirements

Rhode Island corporations and qualified foreign corporations must file an annual report. Annual reports are not available on the secretary of state's website. The filing fee is $50.

Corporate Taxes

Rhode Island corporations and qualified foreign corporations must pay an income tax. The tax rate is 9 percent of net income attributable to Rhode Island. In addition, Rhode Island corporations and qualified foreign corporations must pay a franchise tax of $2.50 for each $10,000 of authorized capital. Authorized capital is the total authorized shares multiplied by the shares' par value. No par stock is valued at $100 per share. The minimum franchise tax is $250.

Tax Forms: http://www.tax.state.ri.us/

S Corporations

Rhode Island recognizes the federal S corporation provision. The Subchapter S election is automatic and no state-specific forms need be filed to make the Subchapter S election.

South Carolina

South Carolina Secretary of State
Edgar Brown Building
P.O. Box 11350
Columbia, SC 22211
(803) 734-2158
http://www.scsos.com/

Incorporating Fee

The fee for filing articles of incorporation is $135.

Name Reservation

South Carolina incorporators may reserve a corporate name by filing an Application to Reserve Corporate Name with the South Carolina Secretary of State accompanied by a $10 filing fee. The name reservation remains effective for 120 days.

Corporate Forms: http://www.scsos.com/forms.htm

Periodic Reporting Requirements

Annual reports are not filed with the secretary of state's office, they are included in a corporation's tax filings and filed with the South Carolina Department of Revenue.

Corporate Taxes

South Carolina corporations and foreign corporations doing business in South Carolina must pay an annual license tax of .001 times their capital stock and paid-in-surplus, plus $15. The license tax is payable by the original due date for filing the income tax return and is paid along with the return or the request for an extension for filing the income tax return. The initial license tax is $25 and is paid at the time of incorporation or at the time of qualification by a foreign corporation. In addition, South Carolina corporations and foreign corporations doing business in South Carolina must pay an income tax equal to 5 percent of a corporation's net income attributable to South Carolina.

Tax Forms: http://www.sctax.org/frames/frameform.html

S Corporations

South Carolina recognizes the federal S corporation provision. The Subchapter S election is automatic and no state-specific forms need be filed to make the Subchapter S election.

South Dakota

South Dakota Secretary of State
Capitol Building
500 East Capitol Avenue, Suite 204
Pierre, SD 57501-5070
(605) 773-4845
http://www.state.sd.us/sos/sos.htm

The minimum fee for filing articles of incorporation is $90 for corporations with an authorized capital of up to $25,000. Authorized capital is the total authorized shares multiplied by the shares' par value. See the sample articles of incorporation on the secretary of state's website for a fee schedule.

Incorporating Fee

South Dakota incorporators may reserve a corporate name by filing an Application for Reservation of Name with the South Dakota Secretary of State accompanied by a $15 filing fee. The name reservation remains effective for 120 days.

Name Reservation

Corporate Forms: http://www.state.sd.us/sos/Corporations/forms.htm

South Dakota corporations must file a domestic annual report. The filing fee is $25. Qualified foreign corporations must file a foreign annual report. The filing fee is $25.

Periodic Reporting Requirements

South Dakota does not have a corporate or personal income tax. South Dakota corporations and qualified foreign corporations may be subject to a sales and use tax.

Corporate Taxes

Tax Forms: http://www.state.sd.us/revenue/forms.htm

South Dakota recognizes the federal S corporation provision. The Subchapter S election is automatic and no state-specific forms need be filed to make the Subchapter S election.

S Corporations

Tennessee

Division of Business Services
Tennessee Department of State
312 Eighth Avenue North
6th Floor, William R. Snodgrass Tower
Nashville, TN 37243
(615) 741-2286
http://www.state.tn.us/sos/soshmpg.htm

Incorporating Fee

The fee for filing articles of incorporation is $100.

Name Reservation

Tennessee offers informal name availability information by telephone at (615) 741-2286. Tennessee incorporators may reserve a corporate name by filing an Application for Reservation of Name with the Division of Business Services accompanied by a $20 fee. The name reservation remains effective for four months.

Corporate Forms: http://www.state.tn.us/sos/forms.htm

Periodic Reporting Requirements

Tennessee corporations and qualified foreign corporations must file an annual report on or before the first day of the fourth month following the close of the corporation's fiscal year. The Division of Business Services automatically prepares and mails an annual report form to each active corporation during the ending month of the corporation's fiscal year. The annual report filing fee is $20.

Corporate Taxes

Tennessee corporations and foreign corporations doing business in Tennessee must pay an excise tax equal to 6 percent of net earnings. In addition, corporations must pay a franchise tax equal to 25 cents per $100 of corporate net worth.

Tax Forms: http://www.state.tn.us/revenue/tdrframe.htm

S Corporations

Tennessee does not recognize the federal S corporation provision.

Texas

Statutory Filing Division
Corporations Section
Texas Secretary of State
P.O. Box 13697
Austin, TX 78711
(512) 463-5555
http://www.sos.state.tx.us/

The fee for filing articles of incorporation is $300. Note that an existing unincorporated business that intends to incorporate without a change in its name must publish its intent to incorporate in the local newspaper for four consecutive weeks.

Incorporating Fee

Texas incorporators may reserve a corporate name by filing an Application for Reservation of Entity Name with the Corporations Section accompanied by a filing fee of $40. The name reservation remains effective for 120 days.

Name Reservation

Corporate Forms: http://www.sos.state.tx.us/corp/business.shtml

Texas corporations and qualifying foreign corporations must file an initial franchise tax report and Public Information Report within one year and 89 days of the corporation's original filing date. Thereafter, corporations must file annual reports each May 15. The secretary of state mails the annual report forms to corporations each year.

Periodic Reporting Requirements

Texas corporations and foreign corporations doing business in Texas must pay an annual corporate franchise tax. Corporations pay the greater of the tax on net taxable capital or net taxable earned surplus.

Corporate Taxes

Tax Forms: http://www.window.state.tx.us/taxinfo/taxforms/00-forms.html

Texas does not recognize S corporation status.

S Corporations

Utah

Division of Corporations
Utah Department of Commerce
160 East 300 South
Salt Lake City, UT 84114-6705
(801) 530-4849
(877) 526-3994
(801) 530-6111 (fax)
http://www.commerce.state.ut.us/corporat/corpcoc.htm

Incorporating Fee

The fee for filing articles of incorporation is $50.

Name Reservation

Utah incorporators may reserve a corporate name by filing an Application for Reservation of Business Name with the Division of Corporations accompanied by a filing fee of $20. The name reservation remains effective for 120 days.

Corporate Forms: http://www.commerce.state.ut.us/corporat/corpforms.htm

Periodic Reporting Requirements

Utah corporations must file an annual Application for Renewal Form accompanied by a $10 fee.

Corporate Taxes

Utah corporations and foreign corporations doing business in Utah must pay a corporation franchise tax equal to 5 percent of income attributable to Utah operations. The minimum tax is $100.

Tax Forms: http://www.e-utah.org/taxhelp.html

S Corporations

Utah recognizes the federal S corporation provision. The Subchapter S election is automatic and no state-specific forms need be filed to make the Subchapter S election. However, Utah requires that a copy of the IRS approval letter be filed with the Utah Tax Commission. S corporations are treated as "Utah Small Business Corporations."

Vermont

Corporations Division
Vermont Secretary of State
Heritage I Building
81 River Street
Montpelier, VT 05609-1104
(802) 828-2386
(802) 828-2853 (fax)
http://www.sec.state.vt.us/

The fee for filing articles of incorporation is $75.

Incorporating Fee

Vermont incorporators may reserve a corporate name by filing an Application to Reserve a Name, available at http://www.sec.state.vt.us/tutor/dobiz/forms/reservat.htm. The filing fee is $20. The name reservation remains effective for 120 days. Vermont offers informal name searches via the secretary of state's website at http://www.sec.state.vt.us/seek/database.htm.

Name Reservation

Corporate Forms: http://www.sec.state.vt.us/tutor/dobiz/dobizdoc.htm

Vermont corporations and qualified foreign corporations must file an annual/biennial report form. You may generate a form online. The fee for domestic corporations is $25. The fee for foreign corporations is $150. For more information, contact the Vermont Secretary of State.

Periodic Reporting Requirements

Vermont corporations and foreign corporations doing business in Vermont must pay a corporate income tax. The corporate tax rate ranges from 7 percent to 9.75 percent. The minimum tax is $250.

Corporate Taxes

Tax Forms: http://www.state.vt.us/tax/download.htm

Vermont recognizes the federal S corporation provision. The Subchapter S election is automatic and no state-specific forms need be filed to make the Subchapter S election.

S Corporations

Virginia

Office of the Clerk
Virginia State Corporation Commission
1300 East Main Street
Richmond, VA 23219
(804) 371-9967
(800) 552-7945
http://www.state.va.us/scc/index.html

Incorporating Fee

The minimum fee for filing articles of incorporation is $75. This includes a $25 filing fee, and a $50 minimum charter fee. The minimum charter fee of $50 applies to corporations with 25,000 authorized shares or less. The charter fee increases by $50 for each additional 25,000 authorized shares or fraction thereof. The maximum filing fee is $2,500.

Name Reservation

Virginia incorporators may reserve a corporate name by filing an Application for Reservation or for Renewal or Reservation of Corporate Name on Form SCC631/830 accompanied by a filing fee of $10. The name reservation remains effective for 120 days.

Corporate Forms: http://www.state.va.us/scc/division/clk/fee_corp.htm

Periodic Reporting Requirements

Virginia corporations and qualified foreign corporations must file an annual report. The Virginia State Corporation Commission mails an Annual Assessment Packet to eligible corporations. Corporations must file their annual report by the last day of the calendar month of the anniversary date of their incorporation. The annual report must accompany an annual registration fee. The annual registration fee is based upon the corporation's authorized shares and ranges from $50 to $850. A table appears at http://www.state.va.us/scc/division/clk/fee_annual.htm.

Corporate Taxes

Virginia corporations and foreign corporations doing business in Virginia must pay a corporate income tax.

Tax Forms: http://www.tax.state.va.us/bt_down.htm

S Corporations

Virginia recognizes the federal S corporation provision. The Subchapter S election is automatic and no state-specific forms need be filed to make the Subchapter S election.

Washington

Corporations Division
Washington Secretary of State
801 Capitol Way S.
P.O. Box 40234
Olympia, WA 98504-0234
(360) 753-7115
http://www.secstate.wa.gov/

The fee for filing articles of incorporation is $175. | **Incorporating Fee**

Washington incorporators may reserve a corporate name by paying a $30 name reservation fee. The form is not available online. Contact the Washington Secretary of State for more information. | **Name Reservation**

Corporate Forms: http://www.secstate.wa.gov/corps/forms.htm

Washington corporations and qualified foreign corporations must file an annual report/corporate license renewal accompanied by a report fee of $50, and a handling fee of $59. The form is not available online. Contact the Washington Secretary of State for more information. | **Periodic Reporting Requirements**

Washington corporations and foreign corporations doing business in Washington must pay a business and occupation income tax that is based upon gross income from activities conducted in the state. | **Corporate Taxes**

Tax Forms: http://dor.wa.gov/

Washington recognizes the federal S corporation provision. The Subchapter S election is automatic and no state-specific forms need be filed to make the Subchapter S election. | **S Corporations**

West Virginia

Corporations Division
West Virginia Secretary of State
State Capitol Building, Room 139-W
Charleston, WV 25305
(304) 558-8000
http://www.state.wv.us/sos/

Incorporating Fee

The fee for filing articles of incorporation is based upon the month of filing. You must visit the secretary of state's website to determine the filing fee.

Name Reservation

West Virginia incorporators may reserve a corporate name by filing Form NR-1, Application for Reservation of Name accompanied by a $15 filing fee. The name reservation remains effective for 120 days.

Corporate Forms: http://www.state.wv.us/sos/corp/startup.htm

Periodic Reporting Requirements

West Virginia corporations and foreign corporations with operations in West Virginia must file an annual report. The Corporations Division mails the annual report to registered corporations. The report is due July 1 of each year. The report must be accompanied by a $10 attorney-in-fact fee and the annual corporate license tax.

Corporate Taxes

West Virginia corporations and foreign corporations doing business in West Virginia must pay a business franchise tax. The tax is based upon the corporation's capital structure. Corporations must also pay a corporation net income tax. The income tax rate is 9 percent. Contact the West Virginia State Tax Department for more information.

Tax Forms: http://www.state.wv.us/taxrev/forms.html

S Corporations

West Virginia recognizes the federal S corporation provision. The Subchapter S election is automatic and no state-specific forms need be filed to make the Subchapter S election.

Wisconsin

Department of Financial Institutions
P.O. Box 7846
Madison, WI 53707-7846
(608) 261-7577
http://www.wdfi.org/

The fee for filing articles of incorporation is $90 for the first 9,000 shares issued; thereafter the fee is $0.01 per share issued.

Incorporating Fee

Wisconsin offers informal name availability information by telephone. Wisconsin incorporators may reserve a corporate name by filing Form 1, Name Reservation Application accompanied by a filing fee of $15. Name reservation is also available for a fee of $30. The name reservation remains effective for 120 days.

Name Reservation

Corporate Forms: http://www.wdfi.org/corporations/

Wisconsin corporations and qualified foreign corporations must file an annual report. The form is not available online. The filing fee is $25 for domestic corporations and a minimum of $50 for foreign corporations.

Periodic Reporting Requirements

Wisconsin has both a franchise tax and an income tax. However, only one tax is imposed against a corporation in a taxable year for the privilege of exercising its Wisconsin franchise or for doing business in Wisconsin. Franchise tax applies to foreign corporations doing business in Wisconsin. The tax rate is 7.9 percent. Income tax applies only to foreign corporations which are not subject to the franchise tax and which own property in Wisconsin or whose business in Wisconsin is exclusively in foreign or interstate commerce. The tax rate is 7.9 percent.

Corporate Taxes

Tax Forms: http://www.dor.state.wi.us/html/formpub.html

Wisconsin recognizes the federal S corporation provision. The Subchapter S election is automatic and no state-specific forms need be filed to make the Subchapter S election.

S Corporations

Wyoming

Wyoming Office of the Secretary of State
Capitol Building
Cheyenne, WY 82002
(307) 777-7378
(307) 777-6217
http://soswy.state.wy.us/

Incorporating Fee

The fee for filing articles of incorporation is $100.

Name Reservation

Wyoming incorporators may reserve a corporate name by filing an Application for Reservation of Corporate Name accompanied by a $50 filing fee.

Corporate Forms: http://soswy.state.wy.us/corporat/profit.htm

Periodic Reporting Requirements

Annual corporation reports are due on or before the first day of the anniversary month of the corporation's initial filing. The report may be drafted and printed online at the secretary of state's website.

Corporate Taxes

Wyoming has no corporate income tax. Wyoming corporations and foreign corporations doing business in Wyoming pay a license tax based upon all assets located and employed in Wyoming. The tax is $0.0002 of the asset value, or $50, whichever is greater.

Tax Forms: http://soswy.state.wy.us/

S Corporations

Wyoming recognizes the federal S corporation provision. The Subchapter S election is automatic and no state-specific forms need be filed to make the Subchapter S election.

Glossary of Terms

Acquisition The purchase of one corporation by another, through either the purchase of its shares or the purchase of its assets.

Administrative dissolution The involuntary dissolution of a corporation by the secretary of state, or other equivalent department, due to the failure of a corporation to meet statutory requirements, such as periodic filing and tax reporting requirements.

Advisory board A body that advises the board of directors and management of a corporation but does not have authority to vote on corporate matters.

Agent for service of process The person or entity that is authorized to receive legal papers on behalf of a corporation.

Alter ego liability Doctrine that attaches liability to corporate shareholders in cases of commingling of assets and failure to observe corporate formalities.

Amendment of articles of incorporation The procedure by which one or more changes is made to a corporation's articles of incorporation.

Annual meeting of directors A meeting held each year to elect officers of a corporation, and to address other corporate matters. Usually follows immediately after an annual meeting of shareholders.

Annual meeting of shareholders A meeting held each year to elect directors of a corporation, and to address other corporate matters.

Apportionment The allocation of income earned from activities in a particular state or assets present in a particular state to determine the tax due in that state.

Articles of incorporation The document which gives birth to a corporation by filing in the state of incorporation. Articles cover foundational matters, such as the name of the corporation, the shares it is authorized to issue, its corporate purpose, and its agent for service of process.

Authorized capital The total number of a corporation's authorized shares multiplied by the shares' par value. For example, one million authorized shares of stock with a one cent par value equals an authorized capital of $10,000.

Authorized shares The number of shares of a corporation's stock that the corporation has the authority to issue. The authorized shares of a class of stock is stated in a corporation's articles of incorporation.

Blue sky laws The securities laws of individual states, collectively. These laws seek to protect people from investing in sham companies—companies that offer nothing more than "blue sky."

Board of directors The directors of a corporation, collectively. The directors of a corporation are its governing board. Elected by shareholders, they vote on major corporate matters such as the issuing of shares of stock, election of officers, and approval of mergers and acquisitions.

Business judgment rule The rule that shields directors from liability for mismanagement of the corporations that they serve.

Bond An interest-bearing instrument issued by a corporation or other entity that serves as evidence of a debt or obligation.

Bylaws The internal operating rules of a corporation, usually set out in a five- to twenty-page document. Bylaws govern such matters as holding meetings, voting, quorums, elections, and the powers of directors and officers.

C corporation Any corporation that has not elected S corporation status.

Certificate of authority A document issued by the secretary or state or equivalent department that authorizes a foreign corporation to operate in a state other than its state of incorporation.

Certificate of good standing A document issued by the secretary or state or equivalent department that certifies that a corporation is validly existing and in compliance with all periodic and taxation requirements.

Close corporation A corporation owned by a small number of individuals. Corporations must elect to be close corporations by inserting a statement in their articles of incorporation. State laws typically permit close corporations to be operated more informally than non-close corporations.

Common stock A corporation's primary class of stock. Common stock holders typically have voting rights.

Conversion or conversion rights Rights allowing the holder of shares of stock or other financial instruments to convert to other shares of stock.

Convertible instrument Financial instruments, such as bonds or notes, that can be converted into shares of stock. Shares of stock may also be convertible into shares of another class.

Corporate secretary A corporate officer, elected by the directors, usually charged with record-keeping responsibilities.

Cumulative voting A system of voting shares of stock used in some states. Cumulative voting gives minority shareholders additional voting power by allowing them to "cumulate" their votes for a single director.

Deadlock The circumstance that arises when either the board of directors or shareholders are evenly split on a vote and cannot take action. Deadlock can lead to judicial resolution of the underlying dispute.

Debt financing A method of financing where the company receives a loan and gives its promise to repay the loan. (See also Equity financing.)

Dilution The effect of reducing an existing shareholder's interest in a corporation when new shares are issued.

Directors The directors of a corporation are its governing board. Elected by shareholders, they vote on major corporate matters, such as the issuing of shares of stock, election of officers, and approval of mergers and acquisitions.

Dissolution The process of shutting down a corporation, settling its affairs, and ending its life.

Distribution A transfer of profits or property by a corporation to its shareholders.

Dividend A share of profits issued to the holders of shares in a corporation. Dividends can be paid in shares of stock or other property, such as shares in a subsidiary or parent company.

Dividend priority Special rights enjoyed by holders of a secondary class of stock that entitle holders to receive dividends before other shareholders.

Doing business as (DBA) A company whose operating name differs from its legal name is said to be "doing business as" the operating name. Some states require DBA or "fictitious business name" filings to be made for the protection of consumers conducting business with the entity.

Domestic corporation In general, a corporation whose articles of incorporation are filed in the state in which it operates and maintains its principal office.

Equity interest Another term for an ownership interest in a company.

Equity financing A method of financing where a company issues shares of its stock and receives money. (See also Debt financing.)

Fictitious business name A company whose operating name differs from its legal name is said to be doing business under a fictitious business name. Some states require DBA (doing business as) or fictitious business name filings to be made for the protection of consumers conducting business with the entity.

Fiduciary relationship A special relationship in which one party, the fiduciary, owes heightened duties of good faith and responsibility to the other party.

Foreign corporation In general, a corporation that operates in one state but whose articles of incorporation are filed in another state; the state in which it operates refers out-of-state corporations as "foreign." The term also refers to corporations chartered in foreign nations.

Franchise tax A tax levied in consideration for the privilege of either incorporating or qualifying to do business in a state. A franchise tax may be based upon income, assets, outstanding shares, or a combination.

Fully reporting company A public company that is subject to the Securities and Exchange Commission's (SEC) periodic reporting requirements.

Go public The process of becoming a public, fully reporting company either by filing a registrations statement with the SEC, or by merging with a public company.

Good standing A state a corporation enjoys when it is in full compliance with the law.

Illiquidity discount A discount in the value of an interest in a business because of legal restrictions on the resale of such interest.

Incorporator The person or entity that organizes a corporation and files its articles of incorporation. The incorporator can take corporate actions before directors and officers are appointed.

Involuntary dissolution The forced dissolution of a corporation by a court or administrative action.

Judicial dissolution The forced dissolution of a corporation by a court at the request of a state attorney general, shareholder, or creditor.

Liquidation preference Certain classes of stock (usually preferred stock) may have a liquidation preference, which entitles the holders to be paid first in the event of the liquidation of a corporation's assets.

Limited liability company (LLC) A new and flexible business organization that offers the advantages of liability protection with the simplicity of a partnership.

Limited partnership A business organization that allows limited partners to enjoy limited personal liability while general partners have unlimited personal liability for the business' debts.

Merger The combination of one or more corporations into a single corporation.

No par shares Shares for which there is no designated par value.

Nonprofit corporation A business organization that serves some public purpose, and therefore enjoys special treatment under the law. Nonprofits corporations, contrary to their name, can make a profit, but cannot be designed primarily for profit-making. Distributions upon liquidation typically must be made to another nonprofit.

Officer The managers of a corporation, such as the president, CFO, and secretary. The officers are appointed by the board of directors.

Outside director An independent member of the board of directors that is not a shareholder or regular employee of a corporation.

Par value The issued price of a security that bears no relation to the market price.

Parent corporation A corporation that either owns outright or controls a subsidiary.

Partnership A business organization formed when two or more persons or entities come together to operate a business for profit. Partnerships do not enjoy limited liability, except in the case of limited partnerships.

Pierce the veil Doctrine that attaches liability to corporate shareholders in cases of commingling of assets and failure to observe corporate formalities.

Preemptive rights Rights enjoyed by existing shareholders to purchase additional shares of stock in the same proportion to their existing holdings.

Preferred stock A separate and/or secondary class of stock issued by some corporations. Preferred stock typically has limited or no voting rights, but its holders are paid dividends or receive repayment priority in the event the corporation is liquidated.

Professional corporation A corporation whose members are all licensed professionals, such as doctors, lawyers, accountants, and architects.

Proxy An authorization by one shareholder giving another person the right to vote the shareholder's shares. Proxy also refers to the document granting such authority.

Qualification The process by which a foreign corporation registers in a state of operation other than its state of incorporation.

Quorum The minimum percentage of either shareholders or directors that must be present at a meeting in order for a vote to be legally effective.

Record date The date by which a shareholder must own a stock in order to receive dividends.

Redemption A repurchase of shares from shareholders by a corporation.

Redemption rights Right of repurchase enjoyed by a corporation that exists for certain shares of stock.

Registered agent The person or entity that is authorized to receive legal papers on behalf of a corporation.

Registered office The official address of a corporation. Typically, this address is the same as that of the registered agent.

Resident agent The person or entity that is authorized to receive legal papers on behalf of a corporation.

S corporation A Subchapter S corporation is a corporation that elects (by filing with the IRS) to be treated as a partnership for taxation purposes.

Secretary (corporate secretary) A corporate officer, elected by the directors, usually charged with recordkeeping responsibilities.

Secretary of state A state official charged with responsibility for the filing of legal documents, including corporation papers. In some states, and the District of Columbia, this responsibility falls upon another department, such as Hawaii's Department of Commerce and Consumer Affairs or Arizona's Corporation Commission.

Securities A broad term that refers to shares of stock, bonds, and some debt instruments.

Shareholder An owner of a corporation and one who holds shares of stock in a corporation.

Shareholders' agreement Also sometimes called a founders' agreement. An agreement between the shareholders of a corporation that can cover various matters, such as a commitment to vote particular persons as directors/officers, guaranteeing owner's compensation, and granting rights of first refusal to the remaining shareholders in the event a shareholder desires to sell his interest in the corporation.

Shelf corporation A fully formed corporation without operations, assets, or liabilities that remains in inventory, or on a "shelf," waiting for a buyer. A shelf corporation can be operating within hours, and uses its original formation date.

Simple majority With respect to shareholder and director voting, more than 50 percent.

Sole proprietorship Simply, a business owned and managed by one person. Sole proprietorships do not enjoy liability protection.

Special meeting of directors A meeting of directors, but not an annual meeting, called for a specific purpose.

Special meeting of shareholders A meeting of shareholders, but not an annual meeting, called for a specific purpose.

Stockholder An owner of a corporation and one who holds shares of stock in a corporation.

Subscriber A person who contracts to purchase the shares of a corporation.

Subscription agreement A contract to purchase the shares of a corporation.

Subsidiary A corporation that is owned outright or controlled by a parent corporation.

Supermajority With respect to shareholder and director voting, any required percentage higher than 50 percent.

Undercapitalization The condition that exists when a company does not have enough cash to carry on its business and pay its creditors.

Voluntary dissolution The intentional dissolution of a corporation by its own management.

Voting right The right enjoyed by shareholders to vote their shares.

Warrant An instrument which grants its holder the option or right to purchase shares of stock at a future date at a specific price. Warrants are tradeable.

Winding up The process of paying creditors and distributing assets that occurs before the dissolution of a corporation.

Written consent A document executed by either the shareholders or directors of a corporation in lieu of a formal meeting.

Index